Building Strategies®
SOCIAL STUDIES

Susan D. McClanahan

Judith Andrews Green

Series Reviewers

▼ **Dr. Pamela Taylor Hakim**
Curriculum Coordinator for
   Distance Learning Program
The University of Mississippi
Oxford, Mississippi

▼ **Faith McCaghy**
Area Literacy Director
Dakota County Literacy Projects
Lakeville, Minnesota

▼ **Bobby Jackson**
Director of Adult Education
Roane County Schools
Kingston, Tennessee

▼ **John Ritter**
Master Teacher
Oregon Women's Correctional Center
Salem, Oregon

▼ **Betty J. Kimberling**
Director of Adult Basic Education
St. Joseph Adult Education Center
St. Joseph, Missouri

STECK-VAUGHN
ELEMENTARY · SECONDARY · ADULT · LIBRARY

A Harcourt Company

www.steck-vaughn.com

Acknowledgments

Staff Credits

Executive Editor:	Ellen Northcutt
Supervising Editor:	Carolyn M. Hall
Design Manager:	Donna M. Brawley
Electronic Production:	Shelly M. Knapp
Cover Design:	D. Childress
Electronic Cover Production:	Alan Klemp
Photo Editor:	Margie Foster
Editorial Development:	McClanahan & Company, Inc.

Photography

Cover: (Grand Canyon) © David Noble/FPG; (Liberty Bell) © Reza Estakhrian/Tony Stone Images; (Statue of Liberty) © Jeffrey Sylvester/Tony Stone Images; p.15 NASA; p.24 (left) Alaska Tourism, (right) © Superstock; pp.28, 31, 36, 38 © Superstock; p.39 © Carol Kohen/The Image Bank; p.45 Culver Pictures; pp.46, 50 North Wind Picture Archives; p.52 The Bettmann Archive; p.54 North Wind Picture Archives; p.56 The Library of Congress; p.59 Culver Pictures; p.60 The Bettmann Archive; p.62 AP/Wide World; pp.63, 64 Culver Pictures; p.65 NASA; p.66 The Bettmann Archive; p.69 UPI/Bettmann; pp.71, 72 Reuters/Bettmann; p.75 © Tony Freeman/PhotoEdit; p.79 © David Joel/Tony Stone Images; p.80 © Superstock; p.82 © Tom Bieber/The Image Bank; p.83 Culver Pictures; p.91 © Bob Daemmrich/Stock Boston; p.92 The Library of Congress; p.94 © Judy Gelles/Stock Boston; p.96 © Keith Jewell; p.97 The White House; p.98 The Supreme Court Historical Society; p.102 Randal Alhadoff; p.103 © David Young Wolff/PhotoEdit; p.106 UPI/Bettmann; p.111 © Tony Freeman/PhotoEdit; p.112 © Markel/Gamma-Liaison; pp.113, 116 AP/Wide World; p.117 UPI/Bettmann; p.118 © Bob Daemmrich/Stock Boston; p.123 © M. Siluk/The Image Works; p.125 © Tom McCarthy/Unicorn Stock Photos; p.128 © Jeffry Myers/Stock Boston; p.129 © Tom McCarthy/Unicorn Stock Photos; p.130 (left) © Tony Freemann/PhotoEdit, (right) Eric R. Berndt/Unicorn Stock Photos; p.131 © Daniel J. Olson/Unicorn Stock Photos; p.135 © Michael Newman/PhotoEdit; p.137 (left) © Myrleen Ferguson/PhotoEdit, (right) © Robert Brenner/PhotoEdit; p.138 © Hazel Hankin/Stock Boston; p.141 (top) © David Young Wolff/PhotoEdit, (bottom) © Michael Weisbrot/Stock Boston.

Illustration

Joe Ruszkowski, page 108: Margery Wunsch for political cartoon. Reprinted by permission of the illustrator. Maps by Maryland Cartographics, Inc.

ISBN 0-8114-6500-4

Building Strategies is a trademark of Steck-Vaughn Company.

Copyright © 1996 Steck-Vaughn Company

Contents

To the Learner

In Steck-Vaughn's *Building Strategies™ Social Studies*, you will study geography, history, economics, political science, and behavioral science. You will also practice your reading skills as you use maps, charts, graphs, and tables. This book includes the following features especially designed to help you develop your social studies skills.

Skills Inventories
- Before you begin work, take the *Check What You Know* skills inventory, check your own answers, and fill out the *Skills Preview Chart*. There you will see which skills you already know and which skills you need to practice in this book.
- After you finish the last practice page, take the *Check What You've Learned* skills inventory, check your answers, and fill out the *Skills Review Chart*. You'll see the great progress you've made. Save these inventories in a folder or portfolio.

Strategies for Success
In each unit *Strategies for Success* sections give you tips and practice for ways to improve your reading skills immediately as you read social studies content. Reviewing these strategies from time to time will help you work through the book.

Thinking and Writing
On the *Thinking and Writing* pages, you will apply your reading and social studies skills while writing your opinions on various interesting topics. Save these examples of your writing in a folder or portfolio and later review how much you have accomplished.

Practice Pages
A *Practice* page follows each lesson. These pages contain a variety of exercises such as vocabulary in context, finding details, making inferences, and reading maps. Check your own work after finishing the exercises to find out how well you understood the lesson.

Extension
Information on topics related to the lesson appears periodically in *Extension* activities. These activities give interesting and helpful additional information. You'll have a chance to give your opinions here.

Glossary

The glossary at the back of the book lists and defines the social studies terms in *Building Strategies™ Social Studies*. It also tells you the page number on which each term first appears.

Answers and Explanations

This section gives you the answers to all the questions so you can check your own work. Sample answers are usually given for open-ended questions that have no one right answer. Answers to multiple-choice questions also explain why one choice is correct and why the other possible answer choices are incorrect. Studying the explanations can help you sharpen your test-taking skills.

Tips for Your Success

There are a few tips to making learning easier. Try all these tips and decide which ones work best for you.

Hard Words. You don't have to know every word in this book to understand what you're reading. When you come to a hard word, keep on reading. The rest of the sentence or paragraph will probably help you figure out what the hard word means. Terms in bold letters in this book are explained in the margin. Also, use the *Glossary* on page 152 to review the terms. If a hard word is not in the *Glossary*, look up the word in a dictionary.

Understanding New Subjects. When you are learning a new subject, such as economic trends, understanding comes a little bit at a time. When you read something that seems very hard, put a question mark with your pencil by the part you don't understand. Keep reading to the end of the paragraph or lesson. Then reread the part you questioned; it will probably begin to make sense. Try to connect the information you are reading to the examples on the page.

Preview the Pages and Predict. Study the table of contents, the unit titles and lesson titles, the unit opening pages, and the pictures. Also read the definitions of important terms in the margins of the pages. All these study aids can help you predict what you are about to read and help you understand the information.

Check What You Know

Check What You Know will give you an idea of the kind of work you will be doing in this book. It will help you know how well you understand social studies content. It will also show you which reading skills you need to improve.

You will read passages, graphs, and maps followed by one or more multiple-choice questions. There is a total of 20 questions. There is no time limit.

Read each passage and question carefully. Fill in the circle for the best answer.

Questions 1–2 are based on the following paragraph.

The Dutch started several trade colonies in the New World. In 1626, the Dutch East India Company founded a colony on an island the Indians called Manhattan. The Dutch named it New Amsterdam. In 1664, the English took over the Dutch colony and renamed it New York.

1. New York got its name

  Ⓐ from the Indians.
  Ⓑ when the Dutch bought it.
  Ⓒ before the English took over.
  Ⓓ after the English took over.

2. The colony of New York

  Ⓐ used to be called New Amsterdam.
  Ⓑ was an English colony.
  Ⓒ used to be called Manhattan.
  Ⓓ all of the above

The U.S. government works on a system of "checks and balances." Each branch of the government checks on the other two branches. This balances the power of all three branches. For example, the President, or executive branch, appoints judges, or justices, to the Supreme Court. The Supreme Court is the judicial branch. Congress must approve the President's appointments, however. Congress is the legislative branch. Supreme Court justices have the job for the rest of their lives. New judges are appointed only when a justice retires or dies. When a new President is elected, the President must work with the Supreme Court justices who were appointed by other Presidents.

3. How are the judicial and executive branches different?

Ⓐ The Supreme Court is the executive branch; the President is the judicial branch.

Ⓑ The President is always younger than the Supreme Court justices.

Ⓒ The President and the Supreme Court justices must retire at age 70.

Ⓓ The President is elected and the Supreme Court justices are appointed.

4. Three of these statements are facts. Choose the one that is an opinion.

Ⓐ Supreme Court justices have the job for the rest of their lives.

Ⓑ Congress must approve the President's appointments to the Supreme Court.

Ⓒ The President should consult leaders in Congress before choosing a Supreme Court justice.

Ⓓ The President must work with Supreme Court justices who were chosen by other Presidents.

5. From this paragraph, you can conclude that

Ⓐ the President and the justices might not always agree.

Ⓑ the President and the justices will always agree.

Ⓒ the President and the justices are friends.

Ⓓ both B and C

6. What is the main idea of this paragraph?

Ⓐ The Supreme Court is more powerful than the President.

Ⓑ The U.S. government has a system of checks and balances.

Ⓒ Congress must approve the President's appointments.

Ⓓ Supreme Court justices are appointed for life.

Question 7 is based on the following map.

North American Deserts

7. You would use this map to find

Ⓐ the average temperature and rainfall in North American deserts.

Ⓑ the types of plants and animals in deserts.

Ⓒ the size and location of North America's deserts.

Ⓓ all of the above

9

Farm, Forest, and Mining Products of Montana

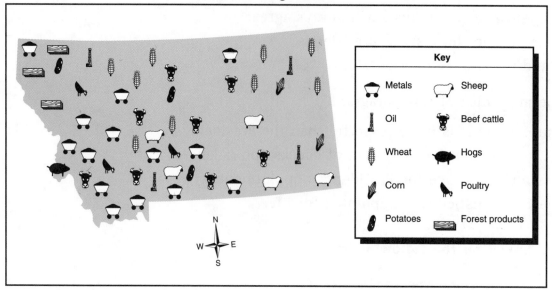

8. Based on this map, you might conclude that Montana is a state with many

   Ⓐ factories.
   Ⓑ farms and ranches.
   Ⓒ forests and mines.
   Ⓓ both B and C

9. Which of the following statements is true?

   Ⓐ Lettuce and strawberries are grown in Montana.
   Ⓑ Most poultry products come from areas where wheat is also grown.
   Ⓒ Metals come from the middle and western parts of Montana.
   Ⓓ There are more hogs than beef cattle in Montana.

10. From this map, you can infer that

    Ⓐ people in the lumber business make more money than ranchers.
    Ⓑ Montana is rich in resources.
    Ⓒ mining is dangerous and dirty.
    Ⓓ all of the above

In the 1980s, President Reagan's administration made some changes to help large businesses. Big companies were charged lower taxes. The government also got rid of some rules about how large businesses should be run. President Reagan thought that helping big businesses would help the whole economy grow. He thought small businesses needed less help than big businesses. As a result, it became harder for small businesses to borrow money, and small companies could not compete with large companies. Later, many people believed that President Reagan's idea that helping big business would help the whole economy did more harm than good.

11. The Reagan administration tried to help big businesses because they thought that

   Ⓐ big businesses needed more help than people did.
   Ⓑ helping big businesses would help the whole economy.
   Ⓒ banks didn't want to help people.
   Ⓓ small businesses couldn't borrow money.

12. Compare and contrast the situation of large and small businesses in the 1980s by choosing the statement that is true.

   Ⓐ The government helped big businesses but not small ones.
   Ⓑ The government helped small businesses but not big ones.
   Ⓒ The government helped both small and big businesses.
   Ⓓ The government did things that made conditions worse for both big and small businesses.

13. Three of these statements are facts. Choose the statement that is an opinion.

   Ⓐ In the 1980s, the Reagan administration lowered taxes for large businesses.
   Ⓑ In the 1980s, it was hard for small companies to borrow money.
   Ⓒ In the 1980s, the government did away with some rules for running large businesses.
   Ⓓ President Reagan's idea that helping big business would help the whole economy did more harm than good.

Questions 14–17 are based on the following passage.

In 1933, Adolf Hitler and his Nazi party came to power in Germany. He wanted to make Germany powerful again. Germany had suffered after losing World War I. Hitler blamed Germany's problems on the Jews and other groups.

Hitler wanted to take over eastern Europe. He wanted to expand Germany's territory. He invaded Poland in September of 1939. England and France agreed to help Poland. Italy agreed to fight on Germany's side. This was the beginning of World War II.

The United States stayed out of the war until December 7, 1941. That was when Japan bombed a U.S. naval base in Pearl Harbor, Hawaii. Then the United States declared war against Japan. Later, Germany and Italy declared war against the United States, too.

Germany surrendered on May 6, 1945. Three months later, the United States dropped atomic bombs on two Japanese cities. Soon after, the Japanese surrendered and World War II ended.

14. You can infer that Hitler invaded Poland to
  Ⓐ expand German territory.
  Ⓑ free Poland from a dictator.
  Ⓒ help Japan.
  Ⓓ help Italy.

15. What is the main idea of the second paragraph?
  Ⓐ Germany invaded Poland in 1939.
  Ⓑ World War II began because Hitler wanted to expand Germany's territory.
  Ⓒ England and France agreed to help Poland.
  Ⓓ Italy agreed to fight on Germany's side.

16. The United States entered World War II because
  Ⓐ atomic bombs were dropped on Japan.
  Ⓑ Germany invaded Poland.
  Ⓒ Germany surrendered.
  Ⓓ Japan attacked Pearl Harbor.

17. World War II ended

   Ⓐ when Germany surrendered.

   Ⓑ when Japan surrendered.

   Ⓒ before the U.S. dropped atomic bombs.

   Ⓓ on December 7, 1941.

Questions 18–20 are based on the following paragraph.

Status is the position a person has in society. There are two types of status. All people are born with the status their family has. Children born into families with low income will begin with a low social status. In an open society, however, adults can reach a second status through education, work, and other achievements. Closed societies don't allow this kind of social mobility, or upward movement. People in a closed society can't change their status through achievement.

18. The main idea of this paragraph is that

   Ⓐ personal achievement is important.

   Ⓑ children in low-income families have low status.

   Ⓒ closed and open societies are different.

   Ⓓ education can change status.

19. Which of the following might be a summary of this paragraph?

   Ⓐ People who live in open societies are happier than those in closed societies because they can change their social status.

   Ⓑ People in open societies can change their social status, but people in closed societies cannot.

   Ⓒ With hard work and a good education, anyone can improve his or her social status.

   Ⓓ Social status is a bad idea and should be banned.

20. People in a closed society

   Ⓐ can change their status through personal achievement.

   Ⓑ aren't born with the same status as their parents.

   Ⓒ can't change the social status they are born with.

   Ⓓ all have the same social status.

When you finish *Check What You Know*, check your answers on page 157. Then complete the chart on page 14.

Check What You Know

The chart shows you which skills you need to study. Reread each question you missed. Then look at the appropriate pages of the book for help in figuring out the right answers.

Skills Preview Chart

Skills	Questions	Pages
The test, like this book, focuses on the skills below.	Check (√) the questions you missed.	Preview what you will learn in this book.
Reading Maps	_____ 7 _____ 9	UNIT 1 ◆ Pages 15–44 Strategy for Success Pages 26–27
Making Inferences	_____ 10 _____ 14	UNIT 1 ◆ Pages 15–44 Strategy for Success Pages 38–39
Understanding Time Order	_____ 1 _____ 2 _____ 17	UNIT 2 ◆ Pages 45–74 Strategy for Success Pages 54–55
Compare and Contrast	_____ 3 _____ 12	UNIT 2 ◆ Pages 45–74 Strategy for Success Pages 62–63
Drawing Conclusions	_____ 5 _____ 8 _____ 20	UNIT 3 ◆ Pages 75–90 Strategy for Success Pages 82–83
Cause and Effect	_____ 11 _____ 16	UNIT 4 ◆ Pages 91–120 Strategy for Success Pages 100–101
Facts and Opinions	_____ 4 _____ 13	UNIT 4 ◆ Pages 91–120 Strategy for Success Pages 110–111
Finding the Main Idea	_____ 6 _____ 15 _____ 18	UNIT 5 ◆ Pages 121–143 Strategy for Success Pages 128–129
Summarizing	_____ 19	UNIT 5 ◆ Pages 121–143 Strategy for Success Pages 134–135

Unit 1

GEOGRAPHY

What do you already know about geography? **Write something you know about it.**

_____

_____

Preview the unit by looking at the titles and pictures. **Write something that you predict you will learn about geography.**

_____

_____

Geography is the study of the continents and the countries of the world. It includes the study of land and bodies of water.

In this unit you will learn about:

◆ maps and charts
◆ continents and countries
◆ climate and how it affects us

Using Maps to View the World

One way to learn about the world is to study a map. Most maps are flat and show all or part of the earth's surface. A globe is a round map that shows how the earth looks from space. On a globe, you can see one half of the earth at a time.

Globe showing the Eastern Hemisphere

If you look at a map, you will see that the earth's surface is mostly water. Almost three-fourths of the earth is covered by the oceans. The map also shows the major land areas, called **continents**. The two halves, or sides, of the earth are called **hemispheres**. The map on page 17 shows the Eastern Hemisphere and the Western Hemisphere.

continent
One of the seven large areas of land on the earth.

hemisphere
Half of the world. *Hemi-* means "half." A *sphere* is a ball, or a globe.

The Continents

Eastern Hemisphere		Western Hemisphere
• Africa	• Antarctica	• North America
• Asia	• Australia	• South America
• Europe		

There are many kinds of maps. Each one shows different information. For example, population maps show how many people live in a certain area. Climate maps show how much rain falls in an area. Maps also show how to get from one place to another.

The Continents of the World

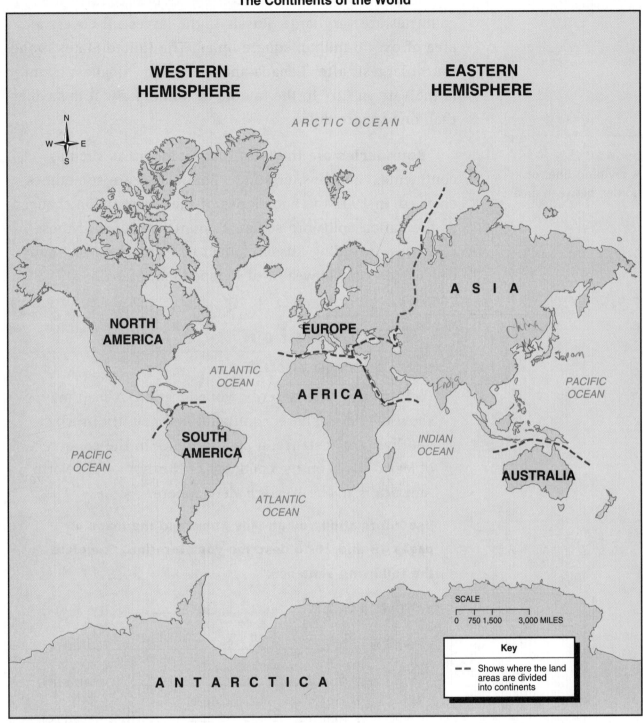

WESTERN
HEMISPHERE

EASTERN
HEMISPHERE

ARCTIC OCEAN

N
W   E
S

ASIA

NORTH
AMERICA

EUROPE

China

Japan

ATLANTIC
OCEAN

AFRICA

PACIFIC
OCEAN

India

SOUTH
AMERICA

PACIFIC
OCEAN

INDIAN
OCEAN

ATLANTIC
OCEAN

AUSTRALIA

A N T A R C T I C A

SCALE

0   750 1,500   3,000 MILES

Key	
– – –	Shows where the land areas are divided into continents

People have divided the continents into countries. Some countries are very large. Russia is the largest. It covers an area of over 6 million square miles. The United States is the fourth largest, after Canada and China. The smallest country is the Vatican City in the middle of Rome, Italy. It is smaller than one square mile.

boundary
A dividing line, or border, between areas.

Boundaries are the lines that divide areas such as continents, countries, or states. Boundaries are sometimes changed. In 1991 the boundaries of the Soviet Union changed as the nation split into separate countries. Some of these countries, including Russia, joined to form a political body called the Commonwealth of Independent States.

◆ Extension

Where Are You?

Maps can help describe your location. A map may show the hemisphere, continent, and country in which you live. For instance, a person living in the country of Mexico lives on the continent of North America. North America is in the Western Hemisphere.

Use information you already know and the maps on pages 19 and 20 to describe your location. Complete the following sentence.

1. I live in _Atsugi Japan_ (city, state),

which is in _Japan_ (country),

which is on _Asia_ (continent),

which is in _Eastern_ (hemisphere).

Write a sentence about a place you would like to visit. Use the name of the city, state, or country.

2. _I would love to see the wild life roaming free on a visit to Africa._

Check your answers on page 159.

Part of the Western Hemisphere: North America

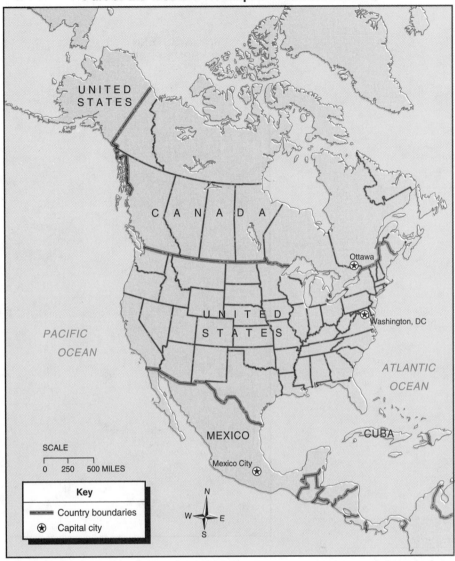

Look at the map on this page. In the bottom corner is a box called the **key**. The key gives you information you need to read the map. The key explains any lines, markings, or symbols shown on the map. For example, the dotted and dashed line shows the boundaries between countries. A star shows where capital cities are located. The four-pointed star is a **compass**. It shows the four directions: north, south, east, and west.

Maps may also contain other information. Some maps use shading or color to show climates in different areas. Other maps may have symbols that show the locations of mountains, cities, or airports.

key
Usually a box on a map that explains what the different lines and symbols on the map mean.

compass
The part of a map that shows the four directions: north, south, east, and west.

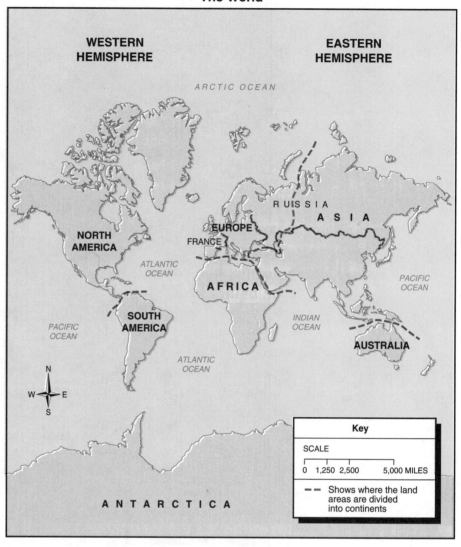

WESTERN HEMISPHERE

EASTERN HEMISPHERE

ARCTIC OCEAN

RUSSIA

ASIA

EUROPE

NORTH AMERICA

FRANCE

ATLANTIC OCEAN

PACIFIC OCEAN

AFRICA

SOUTH AMERICA

PACIFIC OCEAN

INDIAN OCEAN

AUSTRALIA

ATLANTIC OCEAN

N
W · E
S

ANTARCTICA

Key

SCALE

0   1,250 2,500   5,000 MILES

— — Shows where the land
        areas are divided
        into continents

scale

A line in the map key that helps measure the distances on the map.

A map key usually contains a **scale**. The scale of a map is very important. It helps you measure the distance from one place to another. You can use the scale to tell how large areas are. For instance, you can use the scale to measure the distance across Australia. Lay a piece of paper across the distance you want to measure. Make a mark on the paper to show the points that are the ends of this distance. Hold your paper against the scale. Put one mark by the zero, and notice where the other mark falls. The distance across Australia is about 2,500 miles.

The scale also can help measure distances between places. For example, the distance between Europe and North America is about 3,000 miles.

▶ Practice

Vocabulary in Context ◆ **Write the word that best completes each sentence.**

1. A _____key_____ gives you information you need to read a map.

2. The land areas of the earth are divided into seven _____Continents_____.

3. The dotted lines between Europe and Asia on the map show the _____boundary_____ between the two continents.

Reading a Map ◆ **Look at the map on page 20. Write your answers.**

4. In which hemisphere and on which continent is France?

_____Eastern Europe_____

5. Which continent is farthest south?

_____Antarctica_____

Finding Facts ◆ **Choose the word or words that answer each question. Fill in the circle for your answer.**

6. Which covers the largest area?

Ⓐ the oceans
Ⓑ Russia
Ⓒ Australia
Ⓓ North America

7. Which statement is true?

Ⓐ The earth's surface is covered mostly by land.
Ⓑ The earth's land is divided into continents.
Ⓒ A globe is a map that shows three-fourths of the earth at a time.
Ⓓ There are six continents.

Check your answers on page 159.

Using Maps to Study Climate

climate
The average weather conditions in a particular place.

Climate is the kind of weather an area has over a long period of time. **Climate** is not the same as weather. The weather can change from one day to the next. To study the climate of a place, you have to look at the weather over many years. Maps can help you study climate. The map on page 23 shows the world's climates.

People who study climate look mainly at two important things. They look at monthly temperatures. The temperature is how hot or cold the weather gets. The people who study climate also look at **moisture**. They are interested in how much rain and snow falls each year.

moisture
Water in the air that often turns into rain or snow.

absorb
To take up or soak up.

Temperature can affect how much rain a place gets. For example, warm places, such as Brazil in South America, tend to get a lot of rain. That is because warm air **absorbs** more moisture from the ocean and other bodies of water. When the air cools, the moisture falls as rain. Cold places tend to get less rain than warm places. The map on page 23 shows the North and South poles. Very little rain or snow falls there because the air is too cold to absorb much moisture.

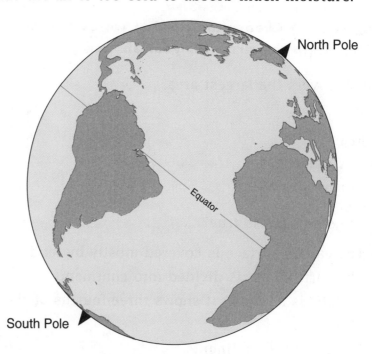

Globe showing the equator and the North and South poles

The World's Climates

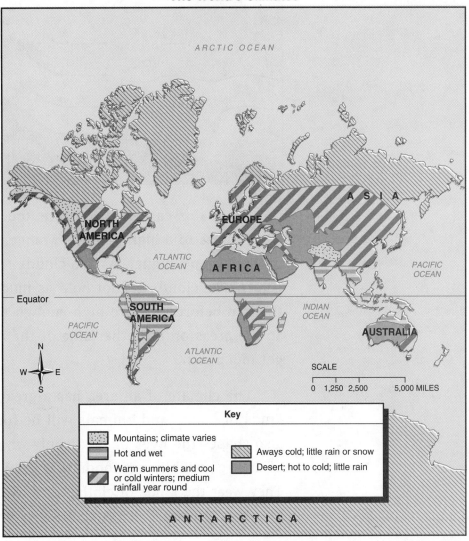

An area's location greatly affects its climate. Nearness to the **equator** or to mountains can affect temperature and moisture. The warmest parts of the world are near the equator. This is because the sun's rays are concentrated in these areas. The farther you go from the equator, the cooler it feels because the sun's rays are not as concentrated.

The oceans also influence climate. In the summer, heat from the sun warms the land more quickly than it warms the ocean. The land near the ocean stays cooler than land farther away. In the winter, the land cools more quickly than the ocean. It holds more of the summer heat, so the areas near the ocean stay warmer in winter.

equator

An imaginary line around the middle of the earth.

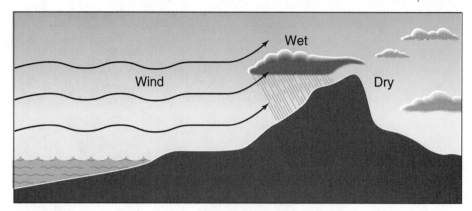

Mountains can affect climate.

Mountains can affect climate, too. For example, if the wind comes to a high mountain range, rain clouds are pushed up higher and higher. As the clouds rise, the air becomes cooler. The clouds cannot hold as much moisture. They drop the rain before they are high enough to cross the mountains. So the areas on the other side of the mountain range never get much rain.

The climate of an area has a great deal to do with what kinds of plants and animals will be found there. The climate also shapes the lives of the people who live there. The people of an area usually eat foods that grow best in their climate. They wear the kinds of clothes and live in the kinds of houses that best protect them from their climate.

People living in very cold areas wear heavy clothes and stay in houses that hold heat.

In desert climates, houses often are made of earthen materials to keep living areas cool.

Practice

Vocabulary in Context ◆ Write the word that best completes each sentence.

1. Areas near the _____Equator_____ are usually warmer than areas farther away.

2. _____Moisture_____ can fall in the form of rain or snow.

3. To study an area's _____climate_____ you have to look at that area's weather over a long period of time.

absorb
climate
equator
moisture

Reading a Map ◆ Look at the map. Write your answers.

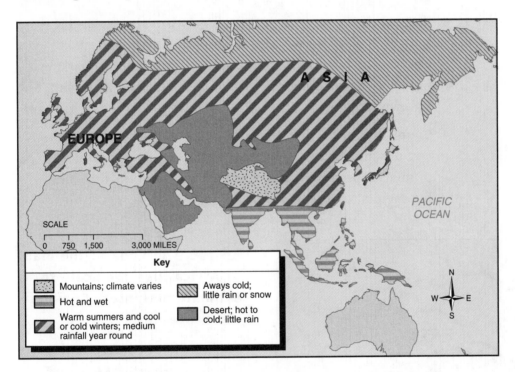

4. Describe the climate in the most southern part of Asia.

   The climate in Southern Asia is mostly Hot & wet _all year round._

5. How would you dress if you lived in the northern part of Asia?

   I would wear a big warm Jacket with a scarf _hat & Gloves, I would wear warm clothes_

Check your answers on page 159.

Reading Maps

Learning to read maps is important. The map key explains map symbols and shaded areas. The key often contains a scale, which can help you measure distances.

❖**STRATEGY:** **Use the scale to find size and distance.**

1. Lay a piece of paper across the distance you want to measure. Put two large marks on the paper to show the points at each end of the distance.

2. Hold your paper against the scale. Line up the first mark with the zero on the scale. Then put a small mark on the paper to show where the scale ends.

3. If the distance you marked is longer than the scale, line the small mark up with the zero on the scale and make another small mark where the scale ends. Continue marking until you have counted out the entire distance between the two large marks.

4. Count the number of times the scale fits into the distance you are measuring. Multiply this amount by the number of miles represented by the scale. This is the total in miles for the distance you are measuring.

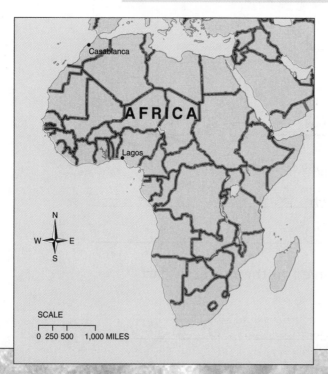

Exercise 1: Look at the map of Africa. Use the scale to estimate distances. Complete the sentences.

1. The distance across the widest part of Africa is about _5,000_ miles.

2. The distance between Casablanca and Lagos is about _2,000_ miles.

Exercise 2: Look at the map of Australia. Answer the questions about its climate.

1. What are the three types of climate found in Australia?

   Hot wet , warm summers cold winter , desert hot to cold

2. Which climate affects the largest area?

   Desert

3. Where is Australia's climate wet? Fill in the circle for your answer.

   Ⓐ in the center
   Ⓑ along the northern coast
   Ⓒ along the southern coast
   Ⓓ along the northern and southern coasts

Australia's Climate

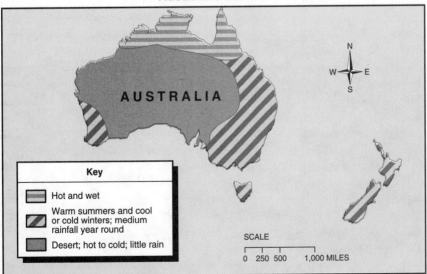

Key

Hot and wet

Warm summers and cool or cold winters; medium rainfall year round

Desert; hot to cold; little rain

SCALE

0   250 500   1,000 MILES

AUSTRALIA

Check your answers on page 159.

North and South America

NORTH AMERICA. There are three large countries in North America: the United States, Canada, and Mexico. North America also contains six smaller countries in **Central America** and many island countries in the Caribbean Sea.

You can see on the map on page 29 that North America has a range of high mountains in the west. These are the Rocky Mountains. There is also a range of lower mountains in the east. These are the Appalachian Mountains. Between these two ranges are wide, flat **plains**. About one-third of North America is covered with forests. These forests are found mainly in the northern part of the continent.

In the far north, the climate is cold all year round. In the south, nearer the equator, it is hot all year round. Most of North America has a variety of temperatures. Summers are warm and winters are cold.

The United States and Canada are rich in oil, coal, and other **minerals**. Mexico has one of the largest oil supplies in the world. The United States and Canada make more than one-fourth of the world's manufactured goods. They sell much of what they make and grow to other countries.

Central America
The countries between Mexico and South America.

plain
A large area of flat land.

mineral
A solid substance, like stone, coal, or salt, that is found in the earth.

The Great Plains of North America

North and South America

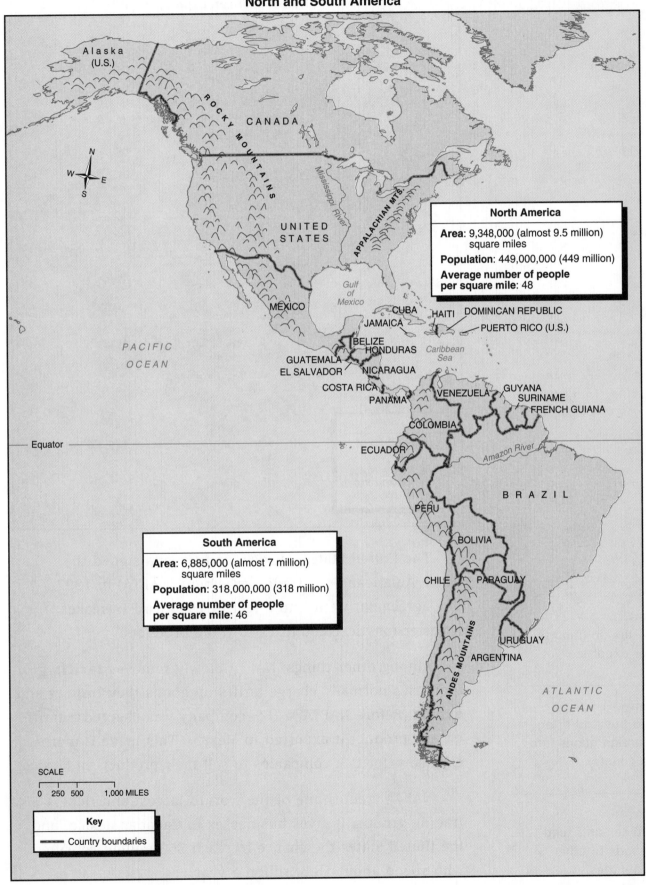

North America

Area: 9,348,000 (almost 9.5 million) square miles

Population: 449,000,000 (449 million)

Average number of people per square mile: 48

South America

Area: 6,885,000 (almost 7 million) square miles

Population: 318,000,000 (318 million)

Average number of people per square mile: 46

Alaska (U.S.)

CANADA

ROCKY MOUNTAINS

UNITED STATES

Mississippi River

APPALACHIAN MTS.

N
W E
S

PACIFIC OCEAN

Gulf of Mexico

MEXICO

CUBA
JAMAICA
HAITI
DOMINICAN REPUBLIC
PUERTO RICO (U.S.)

BELIZE
HONDURAS
GUATEMALA
EL SALVADOR
NICARAGUA
COSTA RICA
PANAMA

Caribbean Sea

VENEZUELA
GUYANA
SURINAME
FRENCH GUIANA

COLOMBIA

Equator

ECUADOR

Amazon River

B R A Z I L

PERU

BOLIVIA

CHILE
PARAGUAY

ANDES MOUNTAINS

URUGUAY
ARGENTINA

ATLANTIC OCEAN

SCALE

0   250   500   1,000 MILES

Key

——— Country boundaries

North American Exports

The United States, Mexico, and Canada signed the North American Free Trade Agreement (NAFTA) in 1992. The agreement went into effect in 1994. NAFTA makes it easier for these countries to trade products.

Among other things, NAFTA slowly removes **tariffs**. Countries normally charge tariffs on goods they **import** and **export**. Before NAFTA, a U.S. company was charged a tariff on any product it exported to Mexico. This made it more expensive for U.S. companies to sell their products in Mexico.

NAFTA creates one of the world's largest and richest trading groups. It gives businesses in Canada, Mexico, and the United States the chance to reach 360 million consumers who spend about $6.6 trillion a year.

tariff
A tax on imports or exports.

import
To buy and bring foreign goods into a country.

export
To sell and send goods to other countries.

fertile
Very good for growing large, healthy crops.

The United States and Canada have large areas of **fertile** land, and they receive enough rainfall for farming. Because of the land and the climate, the two countries produce more food than they need. Much of this food is exported to other countries.

Many of the people in Mexico, Central America, and on the islands in the Caribbean Sea live by farming. Some countries grow only one or two main crops. For example, Honduras grows mainly bananas and coffee. With so few crops, a bad growing season can bring hardship to the whole country.

Because of their beautiful beaches and other attractions, Mexico and some Caribbean countries attract tourists. The **tourism** trade is one of the largest employers in Mexico.

tourism
Traveling for pleasure.

rain forest
A wet tropical forest with tall trees that grow very close together.

SOUTH AMERICA. There are 13 countries in South America. The largest country, Brazil, covers almost half the continent. The world's largest **rain forest**, the Amazon rain forest, covers about a third of Brazil.

Rain forests are important. They contain millions of kinds of plants and animals. Products such as rubber, foods, and some medicines come from rain forests. A medicine used to fight cancer has been made from a tree found in the rain forest.

The Amazon rain forest in northern Brazil

Annual Rainfall in South America

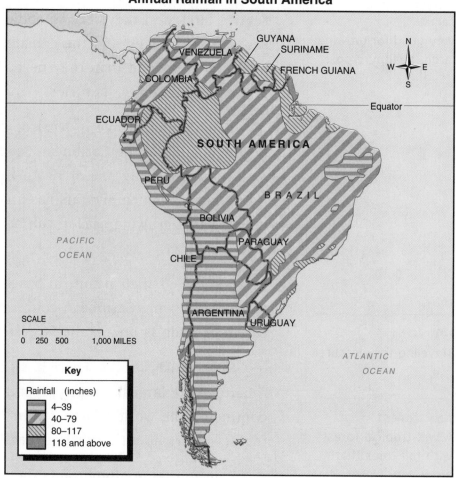

The equator runs across South America, so the climate of much of the continent is warm all year. The continent has grassy plains, farmlands, rain forests, and high mountains called the Andes. The map on this page shows how much rain the continent gets each year.

Many people in South America work on small farms. These farms produce very little food for their owners. The best land often makes up very large farms, which are owned by a few wealthy people. These farms grow beef, coffee, cotton, and other crops for export.

South America has some factories, but many products must still be imported. South America is rich in minerals and other **raw materials**. However, some of these materials are very hard to reach. They are in places where there are few roads and railroads.

raw material
A natural substance, like cotton or wood, from which goods are made.

▶ ## Practice

Vocabulary in Context ◆ **Write the word that best completes each sentence.**

1. The United States and Canada grow enough food to

   <u>export</u> to other countries.

2. Between the mountain ranges are large, flat areas called

   <u>Plains</u> .

3. The best farmland is very <u>fertile</u> .

Reading a Map ◆ **Look at the map on page 32. Write your answers.**

4. Which two countries in South America are farthest south?

   <u>Chile & Argentina</u>

5. What is the yearly rainfall in most of Brazil?

   <u>40-79</u>

Finding Facts ◆ **Choose the word or words that best complete each sentence. Fill in the circle for your answer.**

6. The equator passes through

   Ⓐ North America.
   Ⓑ South America.
   Ⓒ Central America.
   Ⓓ The Caribbean Sea.

7. The two countries in North America that make more than one-fourth of the world's manufactured goods are

   Ⓐ Mexico and Cuba.
   Ⓑ Mexico and the United States.
   Ⓒ Mexico and Canada.
   Ⓓ Canada and the United States.

Check your answers on pages 159–160.

Europe and Africa

EUROPE. Europe is not much larger than the United States, but three times as many people live in Europe. Most of the 48 countries of Europe are very small, but many of them are world powers. France, Germany, and the United Kingdom are countries in Europe. Part of Russia is also in Europe.

Almost all of Europe is near the sea. It has a long, jagged coastline with many good harbors for ships. There are mountains in the northern and southern parts of Europe. The central part is a rolling plain.

Although Europe is quite far north, the winters are usually mild. Even in Norway, which is partly in the **Arctic**, the ocean does not freeze. Look at the map below. As you can see, Europe is kept warm by winds blowing in from the Atlantic Ocean. A warm ocean current called the Gulf Stream flows from the Gulf of Mexico to Europe.

Europe is an **industrialized** continent. It has modern mining, manufacturing, and farming. Europe has **natural resources** like coal and iron. It also has rich soil and good rainfall for crops. Over half the land is used for farming. Europe produces enough food to feed its large population. Europe also imports and exports food.

Arctic
Area surrounding the North Pole and including some of northern Europe.

industrialized
An area that is industrialized has many factories.

natural resources
Things found in nature, such as land, water, forests, and minerals.

The Gulf Stream

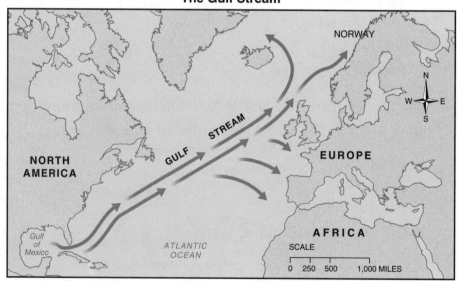

Europe and Africa

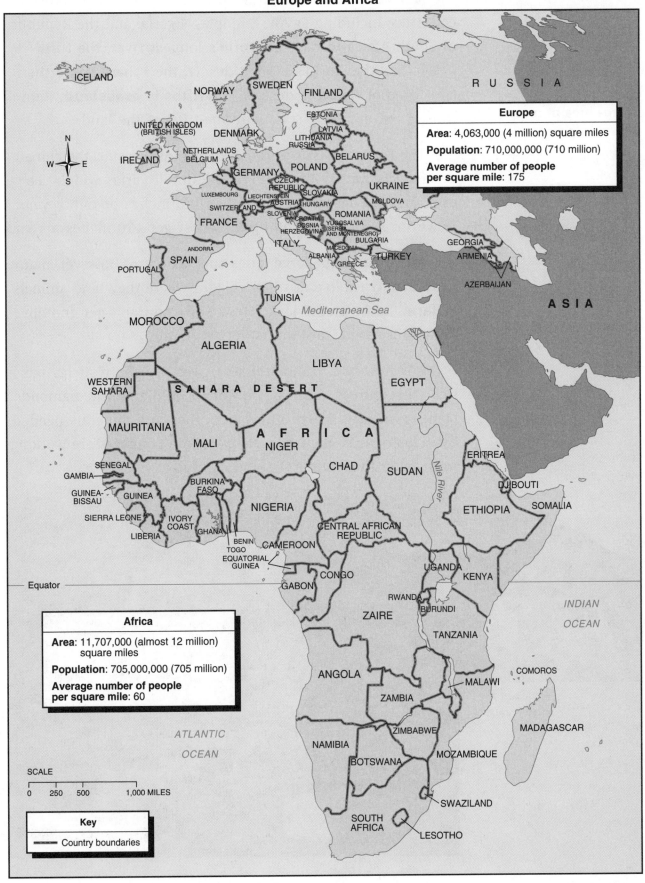

ICELAND

NORWAY SWEDEN FINLAND

RUSSIA

ESTONIA

UNITED KINGDOM
(BRITISH ISLES)   DENMARK   LATVIA
                          LITHUANIA
                          RUSSIA

IRELAND   NETHERLANDS   BELARUS
          BELGIUM
          GERMANY   POLAND
                    CZECH
          LUXEMBOURG   REPUBLIC   SLOVAKIA   UKRAINE
          LIECHTENSTEIN
          SWITZERLAND   AUSTRIA HUNGARY   MOLDOVA
                        SLOVENIA   ROMANIA
          FRANCE   CROATIA   YUGOSALVIA
                   BOSNIA   (SERBIA
                   HERZEGOVINA   AND MONTENEGRO)
                            BULGARIA   GEORGIA
          ANDORRA   ITALY   MACEDONIA
          SPAIN   ALBANIA   TURKEY   ARMENIA
PORTUGAL   GREECE   AZERBAIJAN

ASIA

Europe

Area: 4,063,000 (4 million) square miles

Population: 710,000,000 (710 million)

**Average number of people
per square mile:** 175

N
W   E
S

TUNISIA
Mediterranean Sea

MOROCCO

ALGERIA   LIBYA   EGYPT

WESTERN
SAHARA   S A H A R A   D E S E R T

MAURITANIA   A   F   R   I   C   A
MALI   NIGER   CHAD   SUDAN   ERITREA
SENEGAL   DJIBOUTI
GAMBIA   BURKINA   Nile River
GUINEA-   FASO   ETHIOPIA   SOMALIA
BISSAU   GUINEA
SIERRA LEONE   IVORY   NIGERIA   CENTRAL AFRICAN
               COAST   REPUBLIC
LIBERIA   GHANA
          BENIN   CAMEROON
          TOGO
          EQUATORIAL   CONGO   UGANDA   KENYA
          GUINEA   GABON
                                RWANDA
                       ZAIRE   BURUNDI
Equator
                                TANZANIA

INDIAN
OCEAN

Africa

Area: 11,707,000 (almost 12 million)
square miles

Population: 705,000,000 (705 million)

**Average number of people
per square mile:** 60

ANGOLA   COMOROS
                 MALAWI
         ZAMBIA
ATLANTIC   ZIMBABWE   MADAGASCAR
OCEAN   NAMIBIA   MOZAMBIQUE
         BOTSWANA

SCALE
0   250   500   1,000 MILES

SWAZILAND

SOUTH
AFRICA   LESOTHO

Key

——— Country boundaries

grassland
A large area of grass such as a plain.

AFRICA. Africa is a large continent. It contains over 50 countries, including Egypt, Ethiopia, Nigeria, and the Republic of South Africa. It has the world's longest river, the Nile. It also has the world's largest desert, the Sahara. More than two-fifths of Africa is desert. Two-fifths is **grassland**. Rain forests cover a little less than one-fifth of the land.

The Equator passes through Africa. As a result, the climate of Africa is warm or hot all year. Rainfall varies widely. For example, the deserts get less than ten inches of rain a year. However, some places along the coast get 150 inches a year.

Africa has some large cities such as Cairo. However, many people in Africa live in small villages where they tend animals or farm. Some places lack fertile soil and don't get enough rain. As a result, farming is very difficult.

Africa is rich in mineral resources. Northern Africa has rich oil resources. Most of the world's gold and fine diamonds come from Africa. Africa also has other rare minerals needed by industrialized countries. Many African countries are working to develop their mineral resources fully.

Homes in the Sahara desert

Practice

Vocabulary in Context ◆ **Write the word that best completes each sentence.**

1. About two-fifths of Africa's land is _Grasslands_ , which provides food for grazing animals.

2. Europe is an _Industrialized_ continent, because it has many factories.

3. The _Arctic_ is the area around the North Pole.

Arctic

grassland

industrialized

resources

Reading a Map ◆ **Look at the map of some countries in Africa. Write your answers.**

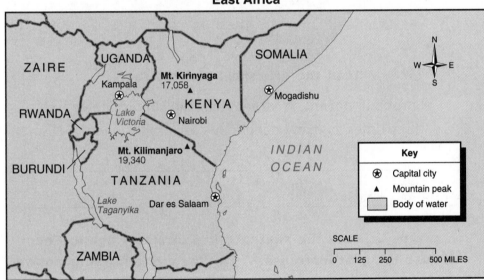

East Africa

4. Which three countries border Lake Victoria?

   Kenya Uganda Tanzania

5. Which country has the highest mountain?

   Tanzania

6. In which country would you find the city of Nairobi?

   Kenya

7. Which five countries have no coastline on the Indian Ocean?

   ZAIRE ZAMBIA Rwanda Burundi Uganda

Check your answers on page 160.

Making Inferences

You make an inference when you combine new information with what you already know. You use thinking skills to make inferences. For example, suppose you know that goods are produced in factories. When you read that Europe produces many goods, you can infer that there are many factories in Europe. You might also infer that many European people work in factories.

❖**STRATEGY:** **Look for facts as you read. Try to connect the facts.**

1. Read each sentence.

2. List the facts supplied in each sentence.

3. Ask yourself: How are these facts related?

Exercise 1: Read the sentence. List the facts.

Europe is not much larger than the United States, but three times as many people live in Europe as in the U.S.

Europe has 3 times as many people than the U.S, even though it is a bit smaller

Exercise 2: Read the sentence in Exercise 1 again. Then choose the best inference. Fill in the circle for your answer.

What can you infer about Europe and the U.S.?

Ⓐ There is probably more open land in Europe than in the United States.

Ⓑ There is probably less open land in Europe than in the United States.

Ⓒ Europe and the United States probably have about the same amount of open land.

Europe has three times as many people as the United States.

Europe - Smaller than U.S
Europe - 3 time as many people as the U.S

> ❖**STRATEGY:** As you read, think about the facts in a passage and what you already know about the subject.
>
> **1.** Look for information in the passage.
>
> **2.** Think about what you already know about this information.
>
> **3.** Ask yourself: How is the new information related to what I already know?

Exercise 3: Read the passage. List some facts you know about deserts. Then write what you know about conditions needed for farming.

Africa has the world's largest desert, the Sahara. More than two-fifths of Africa is desert.

Deserts are hot in the day Cold at night dry not alot of water.

Water is needed to have a productive farm.

Exercise 4: Add the facts in the passage to what you already know. Choose the best inference. Fill in the circle for your answer.

What can you infer about farming in Africa?

Ⓐ Farms cover all of Africa.

Ⓑ Floods are a problem in all of Africa.

Ⓒ Large parts of Africa cannot be farmed.

Ⓓ There is not enough water for farming in any part of Africa.

Exercise 5: List one fact from the passage that supports your inference.

Water is hard to come by n Africa Not enough of it is around for farming

Asia, Australia, and Antarctica

ASIA. The largest continent is Asia. It contains one-third of all the land in the world. Asia is so big that different parts have very different climates. The far north of Asia is very cold. The south, southwest, and southeast are very hot.

More than half of the world's population lives in Asia. Many of the people live in the valleys or along the seacoasts. Southwest Asia includes Saudi Arabia, Iran, Iraq, and Israel. This part of Asia is also called the Middle East. Much of this area is rich in oil.

115°F
115 degrees Fahrenheit in temperature. Water freezes at 32 degrees Fahrenheit and boils at 212 degrees Fahrenheit.

In some parts of Southwest Asia, the temperature can reach **115°F** during the day. As in other areas, some of the people farm and live and work in cities. A few Asians are still nomads—people who move from place to place with their animals. There are about 86 people per square mile in Southwest Asia.

Southern Asia consists largely of India, Pakistan, Bangladesh, and Sri Lanka. The world's tallest mountains, the Himalayas, are found there. Southern Asia has good farmland; however, there are many people to feed (725 per square mile).

Southeast Asia includes Vietnam, Thailand, Indonesia, and the Philippines. This part of Asia is rich in natural resources. It has forests, good farmland, water, and minerals.

monsoon
A wind in southern Asia. It brings heavy rains to this area each year.

In southern parts of Asia, there are seasonal winds called **monsoons**. For part of the year, the winds blow from the land toward the ocean. These winds are dry. Then the winds change direction and blow from the ocean over the land. These winds bring heavy rains.

Eastern Asia contains China, North and South Korea, and Japan. There are about 412 people per square mile in Eastern Asia. Many of the people live in large industrial cities such as Yokohama and Shanghai.

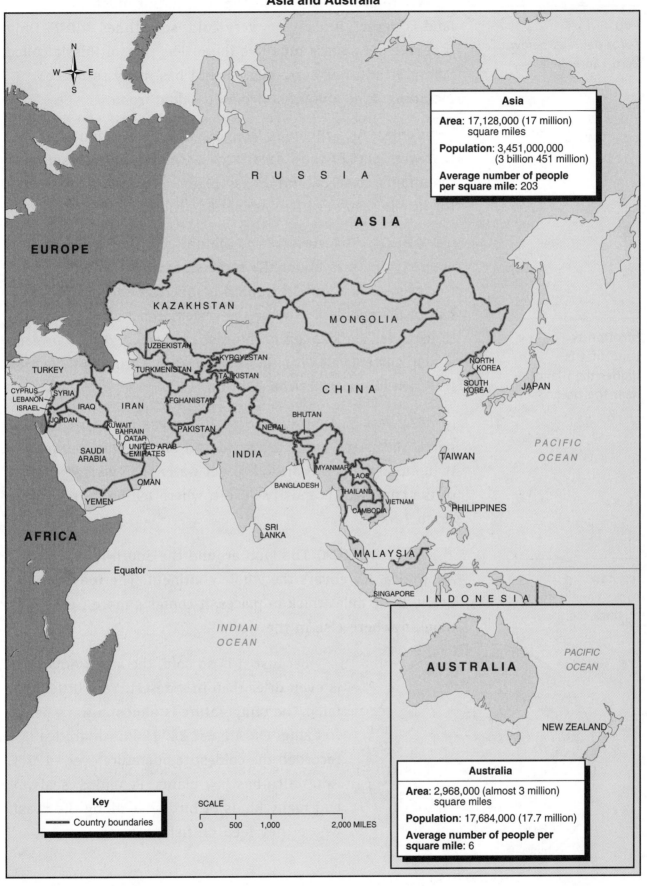

Asia

Area: 17,128,000 (17 million) square miles

Population: 3,451,000,000 (3 billion 451 million)

Average number of people per square mile: 203

RUSSIA

ASIA

EUROPE

KAZAKHSTAN

MONGOLIA

UZBEKISTAN

KYRGYZSTAN

TURKMENISTAN

TAJIKISTAN

NORTH KOREA

SOUTH KOREA

JAPAN

TURKEY

CYPRUS
LEBANON
ISRAEL

SYRIA

IRAQ

IRAN

AFGHANISTAN

CHINA

JORDAN

KUWAIT
BAHRAIN
QATAR
UNITED ARAB EMIRATES

PAKISTAN

NEPAL

BHUTAN

TAIWAN

PACIFIC OCEAN

SAUDI ARABIA

OMAN

INDIA

MYANMAR

LAOS

YEMEN

BANGLADESH

THAILAND

VIETNAM

CAMBODIA

PHILIPPINES

AFRICA

SRI LANKA

Equator

MALAYSIA

SINGAPORE

INDONESIA

INDIAN OCEAN

AUSTRALIA

PACIFIC OCEAN

NEW ZEALAND

Key

—— Country boundaries

SCALE

0   500   1,000   2,000 MILES

Australia

Area: 2,968,000 (almost 3 million) square miles

Population: 17,684,000 (17.7 million)

Average number of people per square mile: 6

Lesson 5

–40°F
Forty degrees below zero Fahrenheit.

There are forests in northern Asia, but much of the land is desert. It also gets very cold, sometimes **–40°F**. Only 6 people per square mile live there. The part of Russia called Siberia lies in northern Asia. Siberia has many resources, including large amounts of oil, coal, and iron.

Central Asia includes Mongolia and some countries that were part of the former Soviet Union. Central Asia has mountains, deserts, and grassy plains. The soil is too poor for farming, so very few people live there.

AUSTRALIA. Australia is the only continent that is a country, too. It is about the same size as the United States. However, only about 18 million people live there. More than half of the people live along the eastern coast or in the nearby **highlands**. The climate in the east is warm, and the farmland is rich. Australia also has the resources needed for its industries. It is rich in oil, coal, iron, and tin.

highlands
Land that is higher than land near the ocean.

The rest of Australia is flat. In the eastern and central parts, sheep and cattle are raised. In many areas, rainfall is light, so wells are drilled to get water. The western half of the continent is mostly desert, where temperatures can reach 120°F.

ANTARCTICA. The land around the South Pole is called Antarctica. Ice covers the whole continent. The **ice cap** is nearly three miles thick in places. It contains more fresh water than anywhere else in the world.

ice cap
A permanent cover of thick ice.

Because it is so cold, the air in Antarctica is even drier than in a desert. Very little snow falls. The temperature is almost always below freezing. On August 24, 1960, Antarctica recorded the coldest temperature ever, –127°F. Antarctica has few plants. Penguins, seals, and many kinds of birds live along the coast, where they feed on fish.

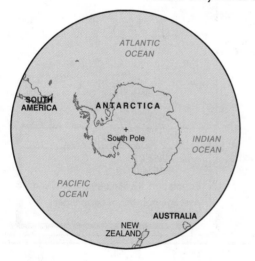

Practice

Reading a Map ◆ **Look at the map on page 42. Write your answers.**

1. Which oceans surround Antarctica?

   Atlantic Pacific Indian

2. What important point is on Antarctica?

   Ice cap

Making Inferences ◆ **Choose the words that best complete each sentence. Fill in the circle for your answer.**

3. Asia is so big that different parts have very different climates. People in different parts of Asia probably

   Ⓐ eat different foods.
   Ⓑ dress differently.
   Ⓒ build different types of homes.
   Ⓓ all of the above

4. More than half of the people in Australia live along the eastern coast or in the nearby highlands. The central and western parts of the country are probably

   Ⓐ sparsely populated.
   Ⓑ crowded and noisy.
   Ⓒ filled with shopping malls.
   Ⓓ important centers of business.

Finding Facts ◆ **Choose the word or words that best answer the question. Fill in the circle for your answer.**

5. What is a monsoon?

   Ⓐ a large continent.
   Ⓑ a desert area that is very day.
   Ⓒ a wind that brings heavy rain.
   Ⓓ a very hot climate.

Check your answers on page 160.

Thinking and Writing

1. Many lessons in this unit explain how to use maps. List four things that a map can tell you about a place.

_____

_____

_____

_____

2. By studying geography, you can learn about people around the world. What can geography tell you about the people who live in an area different from yours?

_____

_____

_____

_____

3. You have read about the climate in different areas of the world. How can climate affect the way people live?

_____

_____

_____

_____

4. If you could live any place in the world, where would you live? Why?

_____

_____

_____

_____

Check your answers on pages 160–161.

Unit 2

HISTORY

What do you already know about United States history? **Write something you know about it.**

_____

_____

Preview the unit by looking at the titles and pictures. **Write something that you predict you will learn about U. S. history.**

_____

_____

History is the study of events in the past. It includes the study of countries, their governments, social conditions, and trade.

In this unit you will learn about:

◆ European exploration of the Americas
◆ events in United States history
◆ the United States as a world power

Europeans Explore America

fifteenth century
The years from 1401 to 1500.

merchant
Businessperson who buys and sells things.

A fifteenth-century ship

settle
To make a home.

Before the late **fifteenth century**, people in Europe didn't know about the continents of North and South America. At that time, Europeans traded with people to the east in India and China. Europeans took things like wood, iron, and wine to India. They brought back spices, silk cloth, jewels, and other fine things. The **merchants** had to travel by land. These trips were hard, and they often took many years. A trip by ship would have been much easier and faster. However, nobody knew an easy sea route to the east.

Christopher Columbus was an Italian explorer. Columbus thought he could reach India by sailing west. The queen of Spain paid for his trip. Spain hoped to increase its trade by finding a sea route to India.

Columbus started his voyage in 1492. It lasted about three months. He landed on an island in the Bahamas. Columbus was so sure that he had reached an island near India that he called this land the Indies.

Columbus made three more trips. He explored the islands of Cuba, Puerto Rico, and Jamaica, and part of the continent of South America. Columbus never found the riches he was looking for. When he died, Columbus didn't know how important his voyages had been.

Soon other Europeans began to explore and **settle** this part of the world. They called the continents of North and South America the New World. Most of the early explorers were from Spain or Portugal.

In 1498, six years after Columbus's first trip, a Portuguese explorer named Vasco da Gama reached India by sea. Unlike Columbus, da Gama sailed east. Later, another Portuguese explorer, Ferdinand Magellan, set out to sail around the world. Magellan was killed in the Philippines. A small number of his crew finished the trip.

Millions of Native Americans were already living in the Americas long before the Europeans traveled there. The Aztecs of Mexico and the Incas of Peru were advanced cultures. The Aztecs built beautiful cities and had many riches. The Incas built a vast system of roads between their cities.

conquistador
Spanish word
for *conqueror*.

In 1521, Spanish **conquistador** Hernando Cortez conquered the Aztecs. Then Spain conquered the Incas. The Spanish took great amounts of gold from the newly-won lands. They also killed or made slaves of thousands of Native Americans.

The Early Explorers

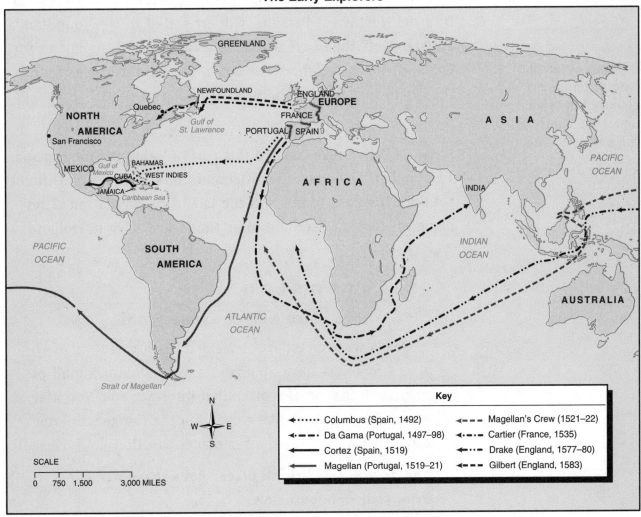

Key

◀······ Columbus (Spain, 1492)   ◀-- Magellan's Crew (1521–22)

◀·--- Da Gama (Portugal, 1497–98)   ◀·-·- Cartier (France, 1535)

◀——— Cortez (Spain, 1519)   ◀·-·· Drake (England, 1577–80)

◀——— Magellan (Portugal, 1519–21) ◀-- Gilbert (England, 1583)

SCALE
0   750 1,500   3,000 MILES

claim
To state one's right of ownership.

challenge
To question or disagree with.

Northwest Passage
A sea route through North America to Asia.

colony
A group of people who settle in another country but remain under the control of the parent country.

At this time, Spain and Portugal agreed to divide the Americas between them. They said that no other country could **claim** land there. Other European countries **challenged** the agreement. They wanted to find a **Northwest Passage** through North America to India. They also wanted land and gold for themselves.

France sent Jacques Cartier to America in search of gold. He landed in Canada near the mouth of the St. Lawrence River. He claimed the area for France. Later, France started a trade **colony** at Quebec.

In the late 1500s, England sent Sir Humphrey Gilbert to find the Northwest Passage. Gilbert sailed to Newfoundland, an island off the coast of Canada. He claimed the island for England. Neither Gilbert nor any other explorer ever found the Northwest Passage because it doesn't exist.

Another Englishman, Sir Francis Drake, reached San Francisco Bay. Drake claimed this part of California for England. The English also started settlements in Virginia. The Dutch set up a fur-trading post on the island of Manhattan. They named it New Amsterdam after the largest city in Holland.

Extension

Where Place Names Come From

Texas was once part of Mexico. As a result, many places in Texas have Spanish names. Look at a map of where you live or of a place that interests you. You may see names that look like words in other languages. You may see places named after places in other countries.

Why do you think these places have these names? Write your opinion below.

_____

_____

_____

Check your answers on page 161.

Practice

Vocabulary in Context ◆ Write the word that best completes each sentence.

1. Spain and Portugal tried to _____ all the land in the Americas for themselves.

2. Other nations, like England, France, and Holland, tried to

   _____ Spain and Portugal by taking land in the New World for themselves.

3. A rug _____ buys and sells rugs.

challenge
claim
colony
merchant

Making Inferences ◆ Choose the word or words that best complete each sentence. Fill in the circle for your answer.

4. In the first paragraph on page 46, *fine* probably means

   Ⓐ plentiful.

   Ⓑ valuable.

   Ⓒ thin.

   Ⓓ cheap.

5. In the second paragraph on page 46, *sea route* probably means

   Ⓐ a way by ship.

   Ⓑ a short trip.

   Ⓒ a way by land.

   Ⓓ a long trip.

Finding Facts ◆ Choose the words that best complete the sentence. Fill in the circle for your answer.

6. The Europeans wanted to find a sea route to India and China because

   Ⓐ they wanted to discover if the world was round.

   Ⓑ they could not get there by land.

   Ⓒ a trip by ship would be easier and faster.

   Ⓓ they hoped to find the Americas.

Check your answers on page 161.

From Colonies to States

found
To start or establish.

trading post
A store set up by merchants or traders.

Pilgrims
A religious group that settled the Plymouth Colony.

debtor
A person who owes money and can't pay it back.

The colonies were **founded** to expand trade for England. English colonies like Jamestown (settled in 1607) and Massachusetts Bay (settled in 1628) were set up to run **trading posts**. The trading posts were owned by merchants in England. These merchants wanted to sell goods to the colonies.

The Plymouth Colony in Massachusetts was founded by the **Pilgrims**. In England, religion was under the control of the king. The Pilgrims left England because they wanted to be free to practice their own religion. The Pilgrims sailed from England in a ship called the *Mayflower*. They lived by farming. They also sold animal skins to European traders.

The English government also used the colonies as a way to solve problems at home. **Debtors** and people who disagreed with the government were sent to the colonies.

The colonists also traded with the Indians.

The Thirteen Colonies

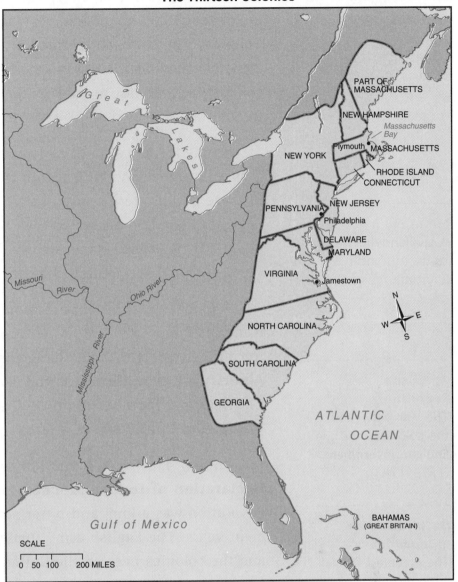

By the 1700s, there were thirteen English colonies in North America. Life in the colonies was hard. The colonists worked for the governor of the colony. The governor worked with the English merchants. The governor and the merchants became rich. The colonists were poor. At first, they weren't allowed to own land or their own homes. However, the laws changed and the colonists were finally allowed to own land.

As the colonies grew larger and richer, the colonists wanted more freedom. Also, the English government raised the duties charged on some products. This angered the colonists. The colonists felt they had the right to set their own taxes.

In 1774, men from twelve of the thirteen colonies met in Philadelphia. This meeting was the first **Congress**. At this Congress, the colonists decided on a plan of action against England. They decided to boycott all English goods. The colonists agreed not to trade with England until they were treated fairly.

People in the colonies began to join together in small groups to fight and win freedom from England. The people in these groups were ready to fight at any minute. In New England, these groups called themselves the **Minutemen**. In April 1775, English soldiers moved into an area near Boston. The colonists felt threatened by this action.

Minuteman
A civilian who was
ready to fight at
any time.

It was at this time that a colonist named Paul Revere made his famous ride. He rode through towns near Boston to call the people to fight the English. The first battle of the **American Revolution** soon followed. The following month, Congress met for a second time. The Congress chose George Washington to lead the colonists' army.

**American
Revolution**
The war between
the colonists and the
English government
(1775–1783).

On July 4, 1776, the thirteen colonies signed the **Declaration of Independence**. However, the American Revolution was a long and bitter struggle. The war lasted eight years. The English army finally **surrendered** in 1783, and the colonies became the United States of America.

**Declaration of
Independence**
The colonies' formal
announcement of
freedom from the
English government.

surrender
To give oneself
or one's army to
the enemy.

*General George
Washington led
the colonists' army.*

Practice

Vocabulary in Context ◆ **Write the word or words that best complete each sentence.**

1. _____ who owed money and

   _____ who wanted to practice their
   religion settled in the English colonies.

2. After the British _____ , the war was over.

> **Congress**
>
> **debtors**
>
> **Pilgrims**
>
> **surrendered**

Making Inferences ◆ **Choose the words that best complete each sentence. Fill in the circle for your answer.**

3. In the last paragraph on page 51, *duties* probably means

   Ⓐ jobs.

   Ⓑ taxes.

   Ⓒ laws.

   Ⓓ punishment.

4. In the first paragraph on page 52, *boycott* probably means

   Ⓐ buy more from.

   Ⓑ sell more to.

   Ⓒ stop trading with.

   Ⓓ meet with.

Finding Facts ◆ **Choose the words that best complete each sentence. Fill in the circle for your answer.**

5. The Pilgrims left England because they

   Ⓐ wanted to get rich in the colonies.

   Ⓑ wanted to be free to practice their religion.

   Ⓒ were debtors.

   Ⓓ were merchants.

6. At the first Congress,

   Ⓐ colonists met in Massachusetts.

   Ⓑ men from a few of the colonies met.

   Ⓒ colonists decided on a plan of action against England.

   Ⓓ colonists signed the Declaration of Independence.

Check your answers on page 161.

Strategies for SUCCESS

Understanding Time Order

When you study history, it helps to know the order in which events happened. You need to be able to recognize the sequence, or order, of events.

Dates and times can help you recognize time order. Also, key words like *before*, *after*, and *later* show time order. The sentences below show examples of time order.

- Columbus began his voyage in 1492.
- Six years after Columbus's first voyage, Vasco da Gama reached India by sailing east.
- Before the Europeans came, the Aztecs had a great empire in Mexico.

❖**STRATEGY:** **Look for key words and phrases.**

1. Look for general time clues. These include words like *before*, *after*, *first*, *second*, *soon*, *then*, *later*, and *finally*.

2. Look for specific time clues. These include words that name days (Tuesday), dates (April 2), years (1836), or times (1:00 P.M.).

Exercise 1: Read the paragraph. Underline key words or phrases that show it is organized in time order.

In 1492, Christopher Columbus began his first trip across the Atlantic Ocean in search of India. After that first trip, he went back three more times. When he died in 1505, he still had not found a route to India. It wasn't until much later that people realized the importance of his discoveries.

❖STRATEGY: **Look for key events or actions.**

1. Identify important events as you read.

2. Ask yourself: Are events listed in the order in which they happened?

Exercise 2: Read the following items. Which of the items is in time order, A or B? Fill in the circle for your answer.

Ⓐ There are two reasons Europeans wanted to find a sea route to India.

    1. They needed India's silk, jewels, and other goods.

    2. They thought that land travel took too long.

Ⓑ For seven years, Columbus tried to find someone to pay for his trips.

    1. He asked John II of Portugal.

    2. He wrote to Henry VI of England.

    3. He met with Spain's Queen Isabella.

Exercise 3: Rewrite the item you chose so that it is a paragraph. Instead of numbering the events, begin each sentence with a key word such as *first*, *then*, *after*, or *finally*.

_____

_____

_____

_____

_____

_____

_____

The Civil War

During the 1850s, the way of life in the North was different from life in the South. One important difference was slavery. Many white people in the South owned black slaves. There were very few slaves in the North.

The main business of the South was farming. Cotton, sugar cane, and tobacco were grown on very large farms called plantations. Many people were needed to work on the plantations. It was cheaper for the owners of the plantations to own slaves than to pay workers who were not slaves.

There were farms in the North, but they were usually small. The main business of the North was manufacturing. Many people worked in factories instead of on farms. Some people were poor, but they were not slaves. Many people in the North spoke out against slavery. Some helped slaves escape from the plantations and move North.

President Lincoln signed the Emancipation Proclamation in 1863.

Northern and Southern States in the Civil War

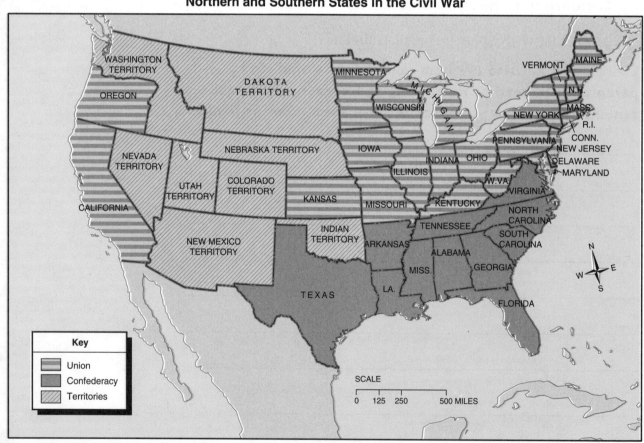

declare
To say publicly.

free state
Any state where slavery wasn't allowed.

secede
To leave a group or organization officially.

Confederacy
The South during the Civil War.

Union
The North during the Civil War.

civil war
A war between two groups of people in the same country.

Emancipation Proclamation
The law that freed the slaves in the South.

segregation
Social separation of different groups of people.

Disagreement between the North and South over slavery grew. New parts of the United States were being settled. When new states joined the United States, each state had to **declare** itself either a **free state** or a slave state. The North did not want more slave states, and the South did not want more free states.

In 1860, Abraham Lincoln was elected President. He had spoken out against slavery, and seven Southern states protested his election. They **seceded** from the United States and set up a new country, which they called the Confederate States of America. Then eight other slave states had to decide which side to join. Four slave states joined the **Confederacy**. The other four stayed in the **Union**.

Fighting broke out between the Confederate and Union armies in the spring of 1861. This was the beginning of the American **Civil War**. Most of the battles of the Civil War took place in the South.

The Union had many advantages over the Confederacy in the war. The Union had factories to make guns, cannons, boots, and other war supplies. The Union also controlled the railroads. The railroads were important for getting fresh troops and supplies to the armies. The Confederacy had problems getting supplies to its troops. The Confederate soldiers did have one advantage. They were fighting the war on their own territory.

President Lincoln wanted to end the war and reunite the country. He also wanted to end slavery in all the states. In 1863, he signed the **Emancipation Proclamation**. This law declared freedom for slaves in the South.

The Civil War lasted four years. In 1865, the Confederate army surrendered and the war ended. The North and South stayed together as one country. Millions of slaves were freed. New laws were passed to give black people the same rights as whites. However, **segregation** of blacks and whites continued for another hundred years.

Practice

Vocabulary in Context ◆ **Write the word that best completes each sentence.**

1. Georgia was one of the first states to _____ .

2. A war between two groups in the same country is called

   a _____ war.

| civil |
| secede |
| **Union** |

Understanding Time Order ◆ **Choose the words that best complete each sentence. Fill in the circle for your answer.**

3. The Confederate States were set up

   Ⓐ when seven Southern states seceded from the Union.
   Ⓑ after Lincoln was elected President.
   Ⓒ after the Civil War.
   Ⓓ both A and B

4. President Lincoln signed the Emancipation Proclamation

   Ⓐ before the Civil War broke out.
   Ⓑ during the Civil War.
   Ⓒ after the Confederacy surrendered.
   Ⓓ during the 1850s.

Finding Facts ◆ **Choose the words that best complete each sentence. Fill in the circle for your answer.**

5. The policy of segregation in the South lasted

   Ⓐ until 1861.
   Ⓑ until 1865.
   Ⓒ for another hundred years after the Civil War.
   Ⓓ until the Confederate states surrendered.

6. The Confederate States of America was made up of

   Ⓐ all the slave states.
   Ⓑ some slave states.
   Ⓒ all the slave states and some free states.
   Ⓓ some slave states and some free states.

Check your answers on page 162.

The Great Depression

The 1920s were a time of great change. New inventions changed people's lives. Cars and airplanes began to make travel faster and easier. The telephone and radio helped people communicate with each other over long distances. Millions of people went to see the new "moving pictures." Many parts of the United States got electric lights for the first time.

The 1920s were a **boom** time for businesses. Americans earned more money than ever before. Many businesses grew quickly and made large profits. Ordinary working people bought **stocks** in big companies. Prices on the **stock market** went up as companies made larger and larger profits. People expected their stocks to make them rich quickly.

In October, stock prices suddenly fell. Many people who owned stocks panicked and sold them. This made prices go down even more. On Tuesday, October 29, 1929, the stock market crashed, or failed. Owners of stocks lost 74 billion dollars. This day is remembered as Black Tuesday.

Banks closed. Many people lost all their savings. Businesses closed, and people lost their jobs and their homes. A time of great hardship began. The United States went into a **depression**. Soon the depression spread to the rest of the world and was called the Great Depression. In the United States, one out of every three people was unemployed.

boom
A time of rapid economic growth.

stock
A share that a person owns in a company.

stock market
The place where stocks are bought and sold.

depression
A long period of severe economic decline.

People stood in bread lines to get food. Many people went hungry during the Great Depression.

During this period, many farmers were forced to sell their farms. Many became migrant workers. They moved with their families from one place to another looking for work.

In 1932, Franklin D. Roosevelt was elected President. He thought of the Great Depression as a national emergency. He had a new plan to help the economy. This plan was called the **New Deal**.

The New Deal included programs to make new jobs such as building roads, airports, and schools. Artists and photographers worked on other government projects.

Congress passed new laws giving the government control of the banks. It also passed laws that helped factory workers and farmers. These laws set minimum wages and work hours. Workers were given the right to form unions. Farmers received government loans to help them start up their farms again.

The government also started the Social Security system and an unemployment insurance program. Both of these programs still exist. Many other laws were made to protect people and businesses. The Securities and Exchange Commission was formed in 1934 to monitor stock trading. Roosevelt wanted to make sure that there would never be another stock market crash or depression.

New Deal
The program created by the Roosevelt government to get the U.S. economy out of the depression.

The New Deal created jobs to help the economy.

Practice

Vocabulary in Context ◆ **Write the word that best completes each sentence.**

1. Buying a share of _____ in a company is a way to buy part of that business.

2. The price of stocks goes up quickly during a

   _____ .

3. As business failures spread to other countries in 1929, the

   world economy went into a _____ .

boom
market
depression
stock

Understanding Time Order ◆ **Choose the words that best complete each sentence. Fill in the circle for your answer.**

4. The Great Depression started

   Ⓐ after the stock market crash of 1929.
   Ⓑ after Congress passed new laws giving government control of the banks.
   Ⓒ in the early 1920s.
   Ⓓ after Roosevelt announced his New Deal.

5. Roosevelt was elected President

   Ⓐ before the Great Depression started.
   Ⓑ on Black Tuesday.
   Ⓒ during the Great Depression.
   Ⓓ after the Great Depression.

Making Inferences ◆ **Choose the words that best complete the sentence. Fill in the circle for your answer.**

6. In the last paragraph on page 60, *monitor* probably means to

   Ⓐ stop.
   Ⓑ televise.
   Ⓒ watch over.
   Ⓓ encourage.

Check your answers on page 162.

Compare and Contrast

To compare means to show how one thing is like another. To contrast means to show how things are different. Comparing or contrasting events or time periods can help you understand history. You can also see how the world has changed. The following sentences show comparisons and contrasts.

- "This grapefruit tastes as sweet as an orange," said Sharon.
- Jeff likes to be with people. However, Bill likes to be alone.
- "Life just isn't the same since we moved from the old neighborhood," said Keith.

❖**STRATEGY: Determine the main idea. Then think.**

1. Decide which ideas or events are being compared or contrasted.

2. Look for key words that show a comparison: *like, as, similar, same, best, worst, better, less, more*

3. Look for key words that show a contrast: *however, but, unlike, different, in contrast*

Exercise 1: Underline the word that best completes each sentence.

During the depression, Americans lived in some of the (same/worst) poverty that they had ever known. It was a time (like/unlike) anything that had ever happened before in the United States. They had no money or food, and many did not have places to live.

Exercise 2: Which of the words that you chose in Exercise 1 showed a comparison?

_____

Exercise 3: Read the paragraph. Underline the key words that help you see a comparison. Circle the key words that help you see a contrast.

In the 1920s businesses made large profits. The 1930s were not the same, however. Business failures were unlike they had ever been before. The depression was just as bad for farmers as for people in the cities. Many farmers lost their farms and were barely able to grow enough to eat.

Exercise 4: Read the paragraph. Underline the things, ideas, or events being compared or contrasted. Circle the key words.

Roosevelt's New Deal was like a rope thrown to drowning people. Government began to play a role in people's lives more than ever before. The government created a safety net that made sure there would never be another depression. Some Americans think Roosevelt was one of the best presidents the United States ever had.

Exercise 5: Use the following information to write a paragraph comparing or contrasting the Great Depression with conditions of the U.S. economy today. Use key words that show comparison and contrast.

During the Great Depression many people went without food and had no place to live. About 13 million Americans were without jobs at the height of the depression.

Franklin D. Roosevelt

_____

_____

_____

_____

_____

A Powerful Nation

Second World War
World War II, fought between England, the United States, and their allies on one side and Germany, Italy, Japan, and their allies on the other (1939–1945).

After the war, factories that had made war supplies went back to making consumer goods.

public works
Projects such as roads, bridges, or dams paid for by the government for the people's use.

welfare
Money paid by the government to people who need help.

After winning the **Second World War** in 1945, the United States became the world's most powerful nation. Many cities in Europe were destroyed because major battles were fought there during World War II. Factories and fields were left in ruins. Other major battles took place in the Pacific Rim countries. Atomic bombs were dropped on two Japanese cities in 1945. Because of such great destruction, the Europeans and Japanese had to rebuild their countries.

The United States didn't have the problem of rebuilding. No battles had been fought on American soil. During the war, American factories had grown rapidly. These factories made ships, airplanes, tanks, and other things used to fight the war overseas. The United States was powerful for another reason since it was the only country that had the atomic bomb.

The United States was powerful economically, too. After World War II, there was a time of economic growth in the United States. Most people had saved money during the war, and now they wanted to spend it. At first, there were not many cars and other goods available. Then, factories that had made war supplies started to make consumer goods. Factories began to make cars, home appliances, and other new products. This business boom created jobs for soldiers returning from the war.

There was a boom in spending by the government, too. After the war, the government spent money on **public works**, health, education, and **welfare** programs. The government created the G.I. Bill. It gave veterans loans to start new businesses.

The bill also helped veterans continue their education. Because some veterans had not finished high school, they could not take full advantage of the G.I. Bill. The GED (General Educational Development) test was started to help these veterans get their high school diplomas.

In the early 1950s, the United States worried about losing its place as the world's most powerful nation. During World War II, the Soviet Union and the United States had fought on the same side. But now the United States felt threatened by the Soviets.

The Americans and Soviets had very different forms of government. Americans felt that the Soviet form of government was a threat to democracy. The Soviet Union wanted to spread **communism**, their type of government, to other countries. In 1949, they helped Communists take over China. The Soviets also spread communism to countries in Eastern Europe. In addition, the Soviet Union had developed an atomic bomb.

The conflict between the United States and the Soviet Union was called the **Cold War**. No real fighting took place. However, the two countries built many weapons. Soon each country had enough weapons to destroy the other.

In 1957, the Soviet Union sent the first satellite, Sputnik 1, into space. A month later they sent up Sputnik 2. Americans feared that if the Soviets could launch satellites, they could also make better weapons. Americans demanded more federal spending for defense. In addition to spending more on weapons, the United States also moved ahead in space research. The United States sent the first American into space in 1961. In 1969, the United States sent the first man to the moon.

In 1969, Americans were the first to land on the moon.

---

communism
A system of government where the state controls industry and business, and all goods are shared equally by the people.

Cold War
The struggle between the United States and the Soviet Union.

After World War II, there was also a boom in population. Americans had just gone through a depression and a war. Many wanted the security of a family. During the 1950s, about 28 million American babies were born. This leap in population was called the **baby boom**.

The baby boom lasted from 1946 to 1964. During that time, the population of the U.S. grew by 75 million. The baby boom helped the country's economic growth. It meant that there were even more consumers to buy American goods.

The baby boomers grew up during a time of plenty. Americans were moving to the suburbs. They were buying cars and other goods. A large number of the baby boomers became the first members of their families to go college.

Today, adult baby boomers make up about a third of the U.S. population. Social scientists still study this group of Americans. Businesses are also interested in baby boomers because they make up a large number of American consumers.

baby boom
A period of increased American births (1946–1965).

After the war, many Americans started families. The rise in population was called the baby boom.

Year	Population
1900	76,212,168
1910	92,228,496
1920	106,021,537
1930	123,202,624
1940	132,164,569
1950	151,325,798
1960	179,323,175
1970	203,302,031
1980	226,542,203
1990	248,709,873

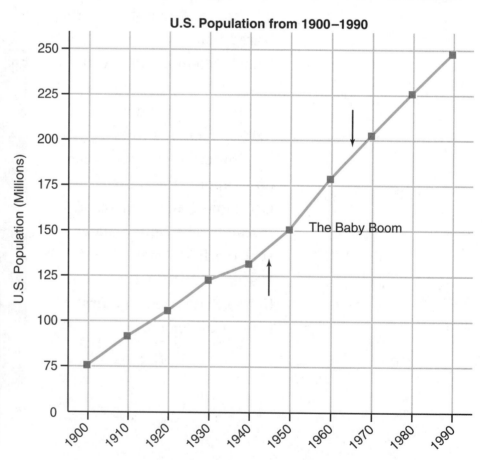

U.S. Population from 1900–1990

The Baby Boom

Practice

Vocabulary in Context ◆ **Write the word that best completes each sentence.**

1. _____ programs give money, food, housing, and health care to people who need them.

2. In a country that practices _____ , the government owns most of the businesses.

boom
communism
welfare

Compare and Contrast ◆ **Choose the words that best complete the sentence. Fill in the circle for your answer.**

3. During World War II, the United States and the Soviet Union fought on the same side. After the war,

   Ⓐ the United States felt threatened by the Soviets.

   Ⓑ they worked together to rebuild Europe and Japan.

   Ⓒ the Soviet Union was no longer important.

   Ⓓ the Soviet Union became the most powerful nation in the world.

Finding Facts ◆ **Choose the words that best complete each sentence. Fill in the circle for your answer.**

4. After World War II, the Europeans and Japanese had to rebuild their countries because

   Ⓐ they were forced to do so by the Americans.

   Ⓑ most of the battles of World War II were fought in the United States.

   Ⓒ their cities, factories, and fields were in ruins.

   Ⓓ they wanted to sell goods to each other.

5. Read the graph on page 66. Between 1940 and 1970, there was a large increase in the U.S. population because

   Ⓐ many people from other countries moved to the United States.

   Ⓑ after the war, many Americans started families.

   Ⓒ fewer Americans traveled to other countries.

   Ⓓ the government encouraged people to have children.

Check your answers on page 163.

The Vietnam War

Vietnam was once a colony of France. The country was taken over by Japan during World War II. When the Germans and the Japanese lost the war, a Communist group called the Vietminh tried to take control. The Vietminh took over most of the north. At about the same time, France tried to reclaim Vietnam. The Vietminh defeated the French. Then Vietnam was divided into two parts. The Communists held the north, and the non-Communists held the south.

In 1957, Vietminh members in the south **rebelled**. These rebels were called the Viet Cong. The North Vietnamese helped the rebels. This was the start of the Vietnam War.

The United States was worried about the war in Vietnam. Some Americans feared that communism would win out and then spread to nearby countries. In 1965, the United States sent troops to help South Vietnam. China and the Soviet Union helped North Vietnam by sending it war supplies.

More than two million U.S. soldiers fought in the Vietnam War. About 58,000 of them died. Millions of Vietnamese were killed. Millions fled the country. Many Vietnamese **refugees** came to the United States.

Americans had mixed feelings about the war. Some thought the war was right. They thought that the United States should use its military might to fight communism. Other people **protested** the war. They felt that the United States should not be involved in the affairs of another country.

Because of protests at home, the large number of deaths, and soaring costs, the United States pulled its troops out in 1973. The North Vietnamese continued their attacks on South Vietnam. Finally, in 1975, South Vietnam surrendered and the war ended. North Vietnam and South Vietnam were joined again. The country became a single state.

rebel
To struggle against authority.

refugees
People who flee a place because of disaster or war.

protest
To fight or speak out against something.

The Vietnam Veterans Memorial shows the names of the more than 58,000 men and women who died in the war.

Unlike World War II, the Vietnam War was not a great victory. There had been much anger about the war. The Vietnam War was especially hard for American soldiers and their families. Many people lost loved ones. Soldiers saw their friends killed. The soldiers came home from the war at different times. There was no victory parade or official welcome for these soldiers. Many wondered whether the war was worth it.

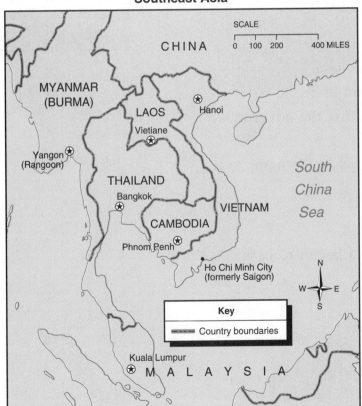

Southeast Asia

The American people are still healing the wounds of the Vietnam War. An important step in this process was the building of the Vietnam Veterans Memorial in 1982. The names of Americans who died or whose bodies were never found after the war are written on the memorial.

Lesson 11

Practice

Vocabulary in Context ◆ **Write the word that best completes each sentence.**

1. Some Americans _____ the Vietnam War.

2. Many Vietnamese _____ had to leave their country.

rebelled

refugees

protested

Reading a Map ◆ **Look at the map. Write your answers.**

3. Hanoi and Saigon were the capital cities of the two Vietnamese nations. Which city was the capital of North Vietnam?

_____

4. Americans feared that communism might spread to countries around Vietnam. China was already a communist country. What two other countries border Vietnam?

_____

Vietnam Before 1975

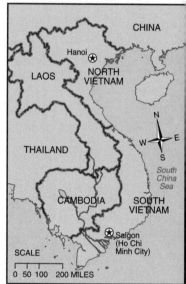

Finding Facts ◆ **Choose the words that best complete each sentence. Fill in the circle for your answer.**

5. The Vietnam War started

   Ⓐ when the Japanese took over Vietnam.
   Ⓑ before the French tried to reclaim Vietnam.
   Ⓒ when the Viet Cong rebelled against the government in the south.
   Ⓓ after the United States sent troops to Vietnam.

6. United States troops left Vietnam

   Ⓐ before South Vietnam surrendered.
   Ⓑ when the Soviet Union and China began to help the North Vietnamese.
   Ⓒ after winning the war.
   Ⓓ when Vietnam became one state.

After the Cold War

Mikhail Gorbachev was president of the Soviet Union when it collapsed.

arms race
A build-up of weapons where one nation tries to have more than another.

economy
The production, distribution, and use of money, goods, natural resources, and services in a country.

revolt
To rebel against authority.

After World War II, Europe was divided into communist and non-communist countries. Most of the countries in Eastern Europe were communist. Germany was divided into West Germany and East Germany. Berlin, the former capital city, was located within communist East Germany. Berlin was divided into non-communist and communist areas, too. In 1961, the East German government built a wall around West Berlin. The Berlin Wall stopped people from leaving the communist part of the city.

Most of the non-communist countries of Europe joined the United States in NATO, the North Atlantic Treaty Organization. The treaty said that these countries would help defend each other. The communist countries of Europe and the Soviet Union created the Warsaw Pact. The nations who signed this pact also agreed to help each other.

Many people feared another war in Europe. The United States and the Soviet Union competed in an **arms race** to have the most powerful and advanced weapons. This was called the Cold War.

In the 1980s, the Soviet **economy** was in trouble. The Soviet Union could no longer afford to keep up the arms race. Mikhail Gorbachev, the new leader of the Soviet Union, made some changes in his country. He allowed people to have more freedom. He also tried to improve the economy. His efforts were not always successful. Many products cost more than they had before. Sometimes there was not enough food.

In 1989, people in many of the countries in Eastern Europe **revolted** against their communist governments. Gorbachev did not try to stop these revolts. Communist governments in Hungary, Poland, and other countries were replaced by democratic governments.

In 1989, Germans tore down the Berlin Wall.

In November of 1989, the German people opened the Berlin Wall. The Berlin Wall had been the symbol of the Cold War. The opening of the wall was a major step in ending the Cold War. In 1990, East Germany and West Germany united to become one non-communist nation.

The changes in Eastern Europe continued. In the early 1990s, the East European nation of Yugoslavia broke apart into separate **republics**. Civil war broke out between groups that had once been part of the same country.

In 1991, Soviet leaders who did not like Gorbachev's **reforms** tried to force him out of office. They were upset that communism had fallen in Eastern Europe. They did not succeed, but their effort left Gorbachev with less power. Republics within the Soviet Union began demanding their freedom. Led by Russia, some of these republics broke away from the Soviet Union and formed the Commonwealth of Independent States (C.I.S.). Gorbachev resigned, and the Soviet Union came to an end.

republic
A country whose leader is elected by the people.

reform
An effort to improve.

 Extension

Where Were You?

When you read recent history, think about what was happening in your own life at the same time. Where were you during the times you have just read about?

Tell what you were doing on these dates:

1989 _____

1991 _____

Practice

Vocabulary in Context ◆ **Write the word that best completes each sentence.**

1. Because the Soviet _____ was in trouble, the Soviets could not afford to keep buying weapons.

2. Russia and other _____ wanted freedom from the Soviet Union.

3. Communist governments in many East European countries fell after people in those countries _____ .

economy
reform
republics
revolted

Time Order ◆ **Choose the words that best complete each sentence. Fill in the circle for your answer.**

4. The Soviet Union came to an end

Ⓐ before the arms race began.
Ⓑ when Gorbachev resigned from office.
Ⓒ when Gorbachev tried to make changes in the economy.
Ⓓ before the the Berlin Wall was opened.

5. The Berlin Wall was opened

Ⓐ during World War II.
Ⓑ when communism fell in East Germany.
Ⓒ when Yugoslavia broke up into new independent republics.
Ⓓ before East and West Germany were divided.

Finding Facts ◆ **Choose the words that best complete the sentence. Fill in the circle for your answer.**

6. Changes in Eastern Europe included

Ⓐ the breakup of Yugoslavia.
Ⓑ the fall of communist governments.
Ⓒ the opening of the Berlin Wall.
Ⓓ all of the above

Check your answers on page 163.

Thinking and Writing

1. History is the study of what has happened in the past, often to a country and its government. Why do you think it is important to study a country's history?

_____

_____

_____

_____

2. In this unit, you read about explorers like Christopher Columbus and Ferdinand Magellan. What personal qualities do you think were important for these explorers?

_____

_____

_____

3. You have read about the American Revolution, the American Civil War, and the Vietnam War. What were the main reasons for fighting each of these wars?

_____

_____

_____

4. Would you prefer to have lived during another period of history, or are you glad to be living today? Explain your answer.

_____

_____

_____

_____

Check your answers on page 164.

Unit 3

ECONOMICS

What do you already know about economics? **Write something you know about it.**

_____

_____

Preview the unit by looking at the titles and pictures. **Write something that you predict you will learn about economics.**

_____

_____

Economics is the study of how goods and services are made and used. It is also the study of how goods and services are paid for.

In this unit you will learn about:

- ◆ how goods and services are made and traded
- ◆ how to read economic charts and graphs
- ◆ how people, businesses, and governments use budgets

Trading Goods and Services

Trade began before history was recorded. To live more comfortably, people traded things that they grew or made for things they needed. For example, they traded food and clay pots for wool cloth. Things you trade are called goods. Services, such as building a house or cutting someone's hair, can be traded, too. The exchange of goods or services for other goods or services is called the **barter system**.

Trade became easier when money was invented. The first money used was probably shells, stones, or beads. Later people began to use metal bars and coins. Then paper money was invented, and it made trading even easier. Paper bills are easier to carry than large amounts of metal or coins.

Everything we produce and trade—food, manufactured goods, labor, and services—has a money value. The value of goods and services depends on how much money people are willing to pay for them.

When there isn't enough of something, we say there is a **shortage**. When there are shortages, prices go up. For example, fruit and vegetables cost more in the winter. That's because they're in shorter supply in the winter than in the summer. When there are shortages of goods and prices go up, businesses try to make more goods. As a result, the supply of goods gets larger. Then the prices start to come down. **Economists** study price changes and try to explain and predict future changes.

The rise and fall of prices is known as the **law of supply and demand**. The law of supply and demand affects your family's buying power. When prices go up, your money buys less. This is **inflation**. For example, the same dollar that bought one pound of rice in 1990 could have bought 4.4 pounds of rice in 1960.

barter system
System of trade without use of money.

shortage
Not enough of something to meet demand.

economist
Someone who specializes in the study of economics

law of supply and demand
The relationship between the supply of goods and the consumer's demand for them.

inflation
An economic situation in which the prices of goods and services keep increasing and the value of money keeps decreasing.

As inflation continues to rise, money buys less and less. People need to earn more money. If wages don't keep up with the rate of inflation, people can't buy as much. Business slows down. Companies cut back and people lose their jobs. This is called a **recession**.

If a recession goes on long enough, it turns into a **depression**. Banks and businesses close. Millions of people lose their jobs. Many people can't pay their rent or mortgage, and they lose their homes.

Many things affect the economy. Wars cause great changes in supply and demand. Wars may create jobs. Wars also cause shortages, which lead to higher prices. People have money to spend, but there are fewer things to buy because the factories make mostly war supplies.

After World War II, there was a shortage of cars, houses, and other goods. As a result, more workers were hired, and more people worked overtime to make enough goods. As people earned more money, they bought more things. The production of goods couldn't keep up with the demand. The shortage of goods and services continued for many years. Eventually, enough goods were made to satisfy consumers' demands. Both wages and prices went up in the process.

recession
A decline in economic activity.

depression
A long period of severe economic decline.

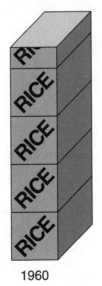

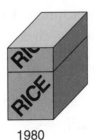

The same dollar that bought 4.4 pounds of rice in 1960 could buy only one pound of rice in 1990.

1960   1970   1980   1990

Practice

Vocabulary in Context ◆ **Write the word that best completes each sentence.**

1. If a recession lasts a long time and gets worse, it can

   become a _____ .

2. An _____ studies how goods and services
   are made and used.

3. A _____ system is a system of trade that
   does not use money.

4. Whenever there is a _____ of a product,
   the price of that product will probably go up.

barter
depression
economist
inflation
shortage

Compare and Contrast ◆ **Choose the words that best complete each sentence. Fill in the circle for your answer.**

5. During an inflation

   Ⓐ wages go up and prices go down.

   Ⓑ prices go up and wages go down.

   Ⓒ wages and prices go down.

   Ⓓ wages and prices go up.

6. During a recession

   Ⓐ businesses grow and jobs increase.

   Ⓑ business slows down and people lose their jobs.

   Ⓒ people have money but there is nothing to buy.

   Ⓓ business slows down and prices go up.

Finding Facts ◆ **Choose the words that best complete the sentence. Fill in the circle for your answer.**

7. The earliest forms of money were probably

   Ⓐ shells, stones, and beads.

   Ⓑ cloth and pottery.

   Ⓒ diamonds and gold.

   Ⓓ goods and services.

Check your answers on page 164.

Productivity

productivity
The amount produced based on the number of people needed to make the product.

You often hear of businesses or factories trying to increase their **productivity**. A business's productivity is based on the number of people it takes to make a product. One company may use 10 workers to make 50 bicycles in a day. Another company may use only 5 workers to make the same number of bicycles. If so, the second company is more productive. When a company increases its productivity, it can sell more products to increase its profits. Productivity is an important way of measuring the country's economic health.

New ideas and inventions have made this country more and more productive. A hundred years ago, one worker might have spent several weeks making a wagon. He would make each part by hand. Then he would put each part in place by hand. Eventually, people figured out how to make interchangeable parts. These parts were made in standard sizes and shapes. Each product was made in exactly the same way with the same parts. Production increased because parts no longer had to be made individually by hand.

assembly line
A line of factory workers and equipment where each worker does a specific job.

Later on, the invention of the **assembly line** for use in factories also increased productivity. One worker no longer built one entire unit. Instead, the product moved along a line in front of several workers. Each worker completed one or two tasks. Then the product went down the line to the next worker until it was completed. Productivity went up because the total amount produced per worker increased greatly.

Today, assembly lines are used to build many kinds of consumer goods.

Henry Ford became famous when he used the assembly line to make cars. He cut the time for building a Ford from twelve and a half hours to one and a half hours. The cost of a Ford dropped from $850 in 1908 to $400 in 1916. As a result, the number of cars on the road increased from 8,000 in 1900 to 8 million in 1920 and to 23 million in 1930. Today there are over 190 million cars in the United States.

robot
A computerized machine that does the same work as a human.

Computers and **robots** have also improved productivity. These inventions have changed the kind of work people do. In the 1970s, factories started to use more machines and computerized robots to do jobs people used to do. Robots can work longer hours than people. They are also cheaper to use.

Using computers and robots means that fewer people are needed in manufacturing. As a result, more people are working in the service industries. Service industries are businesses that perform tasks for people instead of making a product. They include stores, restaurants, travel agencies, and hospitals. People in the service industries use computers, too.

Robots can work longer hours than humans.

◆ Extension

Computers in Your Life

You may use computers without knowing it, since computers are everywhere. If you wear a digital watch, you use a computer. If you get money from an automatic teller machine, you use a computer. VCRs and microwave ovens contain computers. Usually computers save you time or let you do things you couldn't do before.

How do computers help you get things done? Describe one way, such as using the alarm on a watch.

_____

_____

_____

Check your answers on page 164.

Practice

Vocabulary in Context ◆ Write the word that best completes each sentence.

1. The relationship between the amount produced and the number of people needed to make the product is called

   _____ .

2. A _____ is a computerized machine that can do some work that human beings do.

assembly

productivity

robot

Compare and Contrast ◆ Underline the words or numbers that best complete each sentence.

3. Before Henry Ford used the assembly line, it took (one and a half/twelve and a half) hours to build a car, but after assembly lines were used it took (more/fewer) hours.

4. The price of a car in 1908 was ($400/$850). By 1916, the price had gone (up/down).

Understanding Time Order ◆ Choose the words that best complete each sentence. Fill in the circle for your answer.

5. The invention of the assembly line came

   Ⓐ after interchangeable parts were invented.

   Ⓑ before interchangeable parts were invented.

   Ⓒ after robots were invented.

   Ⓓ about the time wagons were invented.

6. Factories started using robots

   Ⓐ more than one hundred years ago.

   Ⓑ in the 1920s.

   Ⓒ when Henry Ford used the assembly line.

   Ⓓ in the 1970s.

Check your answers on pages 164–165.

Drawing Conclusions

When you study economics, you need to draw your own conclusions. A conclusion is a judgment you make after studying all the facts you have. Conclusions are usually not stated directly in a passage. You draw your own conclusion by reading between the lines (figuring out what the facts mean).

❖**STRATEGY:** **Study the facts and read between the lines. Then think it through.**

1. Read the whole passage.

2. Ask yourself: What are the facts?

3. Ask yourself: What are my ideas about the facts and how they fit together?

4. Ask yourself: What do the facts and ideas tell me?

Exercise 1: Read this paragraph. Underline the facts. Think about how they fit together. Then answer the question.

One of the ways that factories use robots is to do dangerous jobs. People should not have to do jobs in which they can be injured. Robots can be used to do high-temperature welding. There may be sparks from the welding, but robots won't get burned. They are made of metal. Sometimes humans can be careless and hurt someone. Robots do what they are programmed to do. You can't say that a robot is ever careless!

Based on the paragraph, what conclusion can you draw about the use of robots in factories? Fill in the circle for your answer.

Ⓐ Robots are smarter than people, so they do a better job.

Ⓑ Using robots reduces the chance of human workers being injured.

Ⓒ Using robots gets more work done in less time.

Exercise 2: Read this passage. Underline the facts. Then answer the questions.

The Great Depression followed a time of economic boom. In 1929, many stocks were worth three times what they were worth in 1924. Then in October 1929, stock prices dropped suddenly. Stock prices continued to fall for the next year and a half. Some people who owned stock had no other form of savings. When the value of their stock went down, they were left without money. As a result, many businesses failed.

Unemployment increased during the depression. In 1930, there were four million unemployed Americans. By 1933, the number had grown to over 14 million. Many people in cities had no money and no jobs. Some people died of starvation. Others left cities to look for work in other places. More than two million people moved from cities to farm areas, hoping to find jobs and food.

The government tried many programs to ease the problems of the depression. While these did help in some places, the problems of unemployment continued through most of the 1930s.

1. What conclusion can you draw about how stock prices changed during the 1920s and 1930s?

_____

2. What facts did you base this conclusion on?

_____

3. What conclusion can you draw about unemployment during the 1930s?

_____

Check your answers on page 165.

Using Charts and Graphs of Economic Trends

chart
Information given in the form of a picture or list.

graph
A drawing that shows the relationship between numbers.

When you study economics, you need to understand many facts and figures. **Charts** and **graphs** provide a lot of information in a small space. They make it easy to compare figures. The chart on the left and the graph on the right show you the same information in different ways.

(Chart)

(Graph)

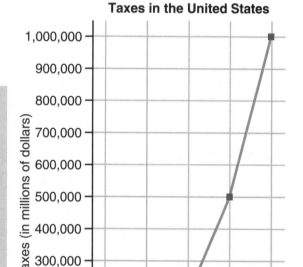

Taxes in the United States

Year	Total Tax* (millions)	Total Tax per Person
1950	$ 39,443	$ 261
1960	92,492	516
1970	192,807	949
1980	517,112	2,278
1990	1,031,321	4,141

*includes individual and corporate taxes, social insurance, excise taxes, estate and gift taxes, customs duties, and federal reserve deposits

column
A list of information that goes from the top to the bottom of a chart.

row
A list of information that goes from left to right across a chart.

In the chart, look at the label at the top of each **column** of figures. The first column says Year. The next column says Total Tax (millions). Next to 1950 you find $39,443. This stands for $39,443 million or $39,443,000,000. The zeros are left out to save space. If you read the chart across a **row**, you can find out the tax for one year. If you read down a column, you can see how taxes have gone up over the years.

The graph uses the same information as the chart. It turns the numbers into a kind of picture. The line on the graph shows you how taxes have gone up or down.

Read the title of the graph. Now read the labels along the side and bottom. As in the chart, the figures are also in millions of dollars. At the bottom left corner, the figures start with 0. They increase by 100,000 million at each line. The dates go across the bottom of the graph. The dates show each ten years as the line moves to the right. The line shows how much taxes have gone up or down over the years.

The graph on page 84 is called a **line graph**. As the line rises or falls, it shows an increase or decrease in numbers. Notice that the graph can't give you the exact figures the way chart did. Sometimes a graph and a chart are printed together. That way you can get both the overall picture and the exact figures.

Another kind of graph is a **bar graph**. A bar graph shows how figures compare in size. The bar graph below compares the number of farm workers to the number of non-farm workers for every ten years between 1850 and 1900. The shading on the bars helps you see which bars represent which workers. It's easy to see that in 1880, for the first time, fewer people worked on farms than other places.

line graph
A graph that uses a line to show an increase or decrease in numbers.

bar graph
A graph that uses bars to compare the size of figures.

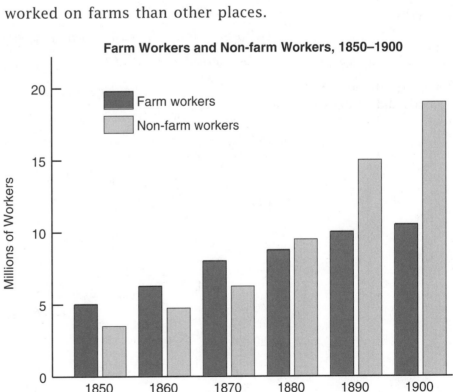

Farm Workers and Non-farm Workers, 1850–1900

Lesson 15

pie graph
A graph that uses wedge-shaped "slices" to compare a part to the whole.

Population of U.S. in 1900

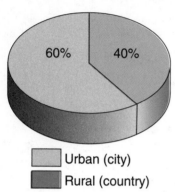

60% 40%

☐ Urban (city)
■ Rural (country)

trend
A general direction of growth or change.

Consumer Price Index
A measure of U. S. inflation which shows changes in the prices of goods and services.

A **pie graph** compares each part to the whole. The whole is always 100%. Each number becomes a slice of the whole pie. It's easy to compare the size of each piece or "slice" to the whole pie and to the other pieces. The pie graph on the left shows where people lived in the United States in 1900. It compares the number of people living in cities to the number of people living away from cities. The total population is 100%.

Charts and graphs often show **trends**. A trend is the direction of change over the years in some part of the economy. For example, a chart or graph might show whether the cost of living is going up or down. Studying trends is a way to get a general idea of what changes are taking place over time.

The **Consumer Price Index** (CPI) measures the average change in prices over time. Economists use the Consumer Price Index to keep track of the changes in the cost of living. The Consumer Price Index is based on the cost of food, clothing, housing, fuel, doctor and dentist's bills, and other basic goods and services. The index compares the costs of these goods and services in different years to their cost in 1982–1984, when the CPI was 100. For example, the CPI in 1990 equaled 130.7. This means that it cost over 30% more to buy goods in 1990 than in 1982–1984.

Consumer Price Index

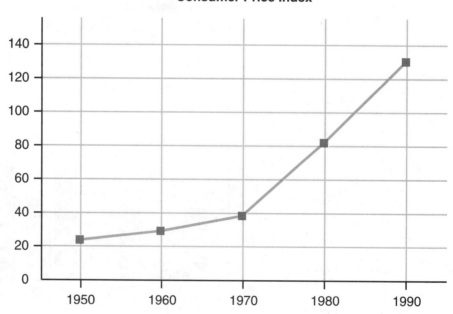

Practice

Vocabulary in Context ◆ **Write the word that best completes each sentence.**

1. A _____ graph compares each part to the whole.

2. A _____ is the direction of change over a period of time.

3. A _____ lists information from left to right across a chart.

| line |
| pie |
| row |
| trend |

Drawing Conclusions ◆ **Look at the two graphs on page 86. Think about the information shown. Then choose the words that best complete each sentence. Fill in the circle for your answer.**

4. In 1900, most Americans

   Ⓐ lived on farms.

   Ⓑ lived in cities.

   Ⓒ worked in factories.

   Ⓓ worked as farmers.

5. Most Americans probably spend

   Ⓐ less money today than they did in 1970.

   Ⓑ less money today than they did in 1980 but more than they did in 1970.

   Ⓒ more money today than they did in either 1970 or 1980.

   Ⓓ the same amount today as in 1980.

Compare and Contrast ◆ **Choose the words that best answer the question. Fill in the circle for your answer.**

6. How is a chart different from a graph?

   Ⓐ A chart usually gives more exact numbers than a graph.

   Ⓑ A chart is better at showing an overall picture of a trend.

   Ⓒ A chart uses bars of different heights to compare numbers, while a graph uses lines.

   Ⓓ A chart usually looks better than a graph.

Check your answers on page 165.

Budgets, Debt, and the Economy

budget
A plan to manage money.

People usually want to save some money. To do this, many people set up **budgets** to manage their income and expenses. They plan their expenses so there will be some money left over at the end of the month. This savings might later pay for a down payment on a house, unexpected medical bills, or retirement.

Businesses must budget, too. To make a profit at the end of the year, businesses try to keep their expenses lower than their income. Then they try to save part of their profit for the future. They may want to use some of their profit to build new facilities, hire new people, or buy new equipment.

Office of Management and Budget
A government agency that manages the money the government collects.

Governments also have budgets. The federal government has an **Office of Management and Budget** (OMB). The President asks the OMB to help prepare a budget for the coming year. This budget goes to Congress for approval. Then Congress votes on which federal programs will receive money and how much money each will get.

deficit
When the amount of money the government spends is more than it gets in taxes.

The government's income comes from taxes. Congress votes on the next year's spending programs before the tax money actually comes in. If the income from those taxes turns out to be lower than the amount of money Congress voted to spend, there is a **deficit**. Then the government has to borrow money to cover its expenses.

A Typical 1992 Federal Tax Dollar

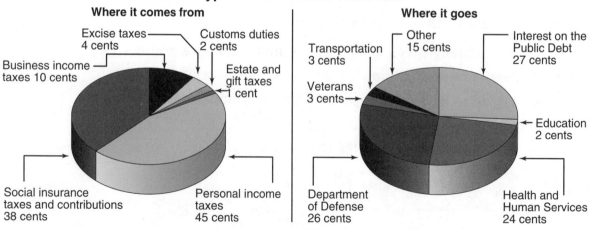

Where it comes from

Excise taxes 4 cents

Customs duties 2 cents

Business income taxes 10 cents

Estate and gift taxes 1 cent

Social insurance taxes and contributions 38 cents

Personal income taxes 45 cents

Where it goes

Transportation 3 cents

Other 15 cents

Interest on the Public Debt 27 cents

Veterans 3 cents

Education 2 cents

Department of Defense 26 cents

Health and Human Services 24 cents

bond
A certificate of debt that guarantees repayment of the loan plus interest in a certain period of time.

interest
The amount it costs to borrow money.

The government borrows money by selling **bonds**. The government pays **interest** to the buyers of the bonds. In order to sell a large amount of bonds, the government has to pay high interest rates.

When the government interest rates go up, all other interest rates go up, too. Banks have to compete with the government for people's money. If the government pays ten percent interest on its bonds, banks then have to pay ten percent interest on savings accounts. Banks also charge interest on the money they lend. They use this money to pay interest on savings accounts. Raising the interest on savings accounts also raises the interest for borrowing money. Therefore, banks might charge twelve percent interest to borrowers.

Sometimes people, businesses, or governments borrow more money than they can pay back. When this happens, banks start charging a higher interest rate, or they stop lending money completely. Sooner or later, spending stops, the economy slows down, and a recession begins. A recession lasts until people, businesses, and government can pay back their debts.

◆ Extension

Government Spending

Out of every $1.00 the government spent in 1990, 26¢ went to the defense department, 19¢ went to health and human services, 2¢ went to education, and 3¢ went to veterans.

Do you think the government should spend more or less in any of these areas? Why?

_____

_____

_____

Practice

Vocabulary in Context ◆ Write the word that best completes each sentence.

1. Before opening a savings account, most people check to

    see which banks pay the most _____ .

2. A _____ helps people manage their money.

3. The United States has been trying to cut spending to

    reduce the _____ .

> bond
> budget
> deficit
> interest

Finding Facts ◆ Choose the words that best complete the sentence. Fill in the circle for your answer.

4. The money the government spends comes from

    Ⓐ interest on the public debt.
    Ⓑ taxes on personal and business income.
    Ⓒ sales of American goods overseas.
    Ⓓ all of the above

Understanding Time Order ◆ Choose the words that best complete each sentence. Fill in the circle for your answer.

5. The Office of Management and Budget (OMB) prepares
   a budget for the coming year

    Ⓐ after the President has asked for a new budget.
    Ⓑ after Congress votes on how to spend money.
    Ⓒ after all the taxes have been collected.
    Ⓓ after taxes have been collected, but before Congress votes.

6. Bank interest rates usually go up

    Ⓐ before the government interest rate goes up.
    Ⓑ after the government interest rate goes up.
    Ⓒ when banks have a lot of customers.
    Ⓓ before there is a deficit.

Check your answers on page 166.

Unit 4

POLITICAL SCIENCE

You hear about politics every day. On the news you hear about Congress raising taxes. Politics and the decisions made by government affect all areas of your life. **Write something you already know about politics.**

_____

Preview the unit by looking at the titles and pictures. **Write something that you predict you will learn about political science.**

_____

_____

Political science is the study of how government works. Government affects our daily lives. It controls many public services like schools and transportation.

In this unit you will learn about:
◆ the United States Constitution
◆ the three branches of government
◆ how the United States makes laws and elects leaders

The Constitution

government
The method of running a country, state, or city.

representative
A person who voices the needs, wants, and opinions of a group of people.

Constitution
The document that outlines the system and laws of the United States government.

After the American Revolution, the thirteen states were linked only by a weak **government**. This government had many problems. In 1787, each state sent **representatives** to a convention to try to solve these problems. These representatives decided the states needed a strong federal, or central, government. The representatives made a new plan of government called the **Constitution**. Many heroes of the Revolution, like George Washington and Benjamin Franklin, helped write the Constitution. The Constitution became law in 1788.

The American Constitution is based on certain beliefs. One belief is that government gets its power from the people. People vote for their lawmakers. Another belief is that government and religion should be separated. People may practice any religion they wish, but the government does not favor any particular religion. Another belief is that each state has rights, although the federal government has the power to control the states.

The Constitution was signed in Philadelphia on September 17, 1787.

The writers of the Constitution had to make some compromises. Some of them felt that the federal government needed to be very strong. Others were afraid that the federal government might be given too much power. The federal government united the states into one country. The federal government was given the authority to print money, organize the post office, control the armed forces, direct trade between the states, and declare war.

To control the power of the federal government, the Constitution split it into three **branches**. That way, one branch could keep the other two branches from becoming too powerful.

The Constitution set up a plan of government that still works today. The Constitution has a **preamble** and seven **articles**. All new laws must follow the Constitution's main plan.

branch
A part or section.

preamble
The introduction to the Constitution.

article
A section of the Constitution.

The Preamble to the Constitution with part of the first article

The first three articles of the Constitution give certain powers to Congress, certain powers to the President, and certain powers to the courts. Article four is about states' rights. Article five tells how to make changes in the Constitution. Article six makes the Constitution and the federal laws more powerful than any state laws. The last article declares that the Constitution became law when nine states accepted it.

The writers of the Constitution knew the government would have to change as the country grew. They allowed for additions, or **amendments**, to the Constitution. There have been twenty-seven amendments to the Constitution.

amendment
A change or addition.

The first ten amendments are called the **Bill of Rights**. The Bill of Rights gives many rights to the people and limits the powers of the federal government. Certain rights are also given to the states. The Constitution is based on **majority rule**. Yet the rights of people who disagree with the majority are also protected.

Some of the amendments in the Bill of Rights gave people rights that most Americans now take for granted. For example, we know that we have the right to a trial by jury. The meaning of some of the other amendments is still being discussed today. For example, the First Amendment allows freedom of the **press**. Some people believe that this includes freedom from **censorship** of any kind, but other people disagree.

More than two hundred years after it was written, the Constitution is still a useful plan of government. It protects the rights of the individual. At the same time, it provides a strong central government. The Constitution also allows for change and growth in government as society itself changes. For example, the Twenty-sixth Amendment lowered the voting age to 18 years. This has allowed many more people to vote in elections.

Free speech is protected by the First Amendment of the Bill of Rights.

Practice

Vocabulary in Context ◆ Write the word that best completes each sentence.

1. The thirteen states were united by the federal

   _____ .

2. The _____ is a plan of government.

3. The Constitution can be changed with _____ ,
   but they must fit into the main plan.

amendments
articles
Constitution
government

Drawing Conclusions ◆ Read the question. Write your answer.

4. Why did the people who wrote the Bill of Rights think it
   was important to protect the rights of people who disagree
   with the majority?

   _____

   _____

**Finding Facts ◆ Choose the words that best answer each
question. Fill in the circle for your answer.**

5. The American Constitution is based on which beliefs?

   Ⓐ People of a country should have the power to make
   their own laws.

   Ⓑ Government should have unlimited power.

   Ⓒ States can make laws that overturn federal laws.

   Ⓓ The power of each state should depend on how many
   people live in it.

6. Why did the people who wrote the Constitution split the
   government into three branches?

   Ⓐ There was too much for just one branch to do.

   Ⓑ Three people wanted to govern the country.

   Ⓒ Each branch could keep the other two from becoming
   too powerful.

   Ⓓ Each section of the country had its own branch.

Check your answers on page 166.

The Three Branches of Government

The writers of the Constitution wanted to make sure that the three branches of government shared power. The Constitution spells out the separate powers for each branch. The three branches are the legislative, executive, and judicial branches.

Congress is the **legislative branch** because it has the power to make laws. Congress has two sections, or houses. The two houses are called the **Senate** and the **House of Representatives**. States with few people felt that each state should have an equal vote in Congress. However, states with more people felt that they should have more votes. To make voting fair, the two houses of Congress are elected in different ways.

Each state, large or small, elects two members to the Senate. They are called senators. The Senate has 100 members or "seats." Each senator serves for six years. Every two years, one-third of the senators must run for re-election. As a result, the membership of the Senate changes slowly.

In the House of Representatives, the states with more people have more representatives. The House of Representatives

legislative branch
Congress. It has the power to make laws.

Senate
One of the two houses of Congress.

House of Representatives
One of the two houses of Congress.

The legislative branch passes laws.

census
An official count of all the people in a country.

has 435 members. The members are elected every two years. Every ten years, the **census** is taken. Based on the new census, then the House decides how many representatives can be sent from each state.

Duties of Congress
- makes and changes laws
- collects taxes
- borrows government money
- decides how government money will be spent
- is the only branch than can declare war

executive branch
The President and his or her cabinet. This branch is in charge of making sure that laws are carried out.

The **executive branch** of government sees that the laws are carried out. The President runs the executive branch of the federal government. The President's job is to make sure that the laws passed by Congress are carried out. The President can also propose new laws to Congress. As commander-in-chief of the armed forces, the President is in charge of defense. The President is elected for a four-year term and may be re-elected only once.

Duties of the President
- enforces laws
- appoints people to government jobs
- can direct the fighting during a war
- represents the United States in dealing with other countries
- heads his or her political party

The President is head of the executive branch.

cabinet
The group of people who advise the President.

The executive branch also includes fourteen departments that help to run government. Some of these departments include the Treasury Department which prints money, the Department of Defense which runs the armed forces, and the State Department which handles foreign affairs. The heads of these departments make up the President's **cabinet**.

judicial branch
The courts; the branch of government that makes sure laws are constitutional.

The courts form the **judicial branch** of government. The most powerful, or highest, court is the Supreme Court. There are nine Supreme Court judges, called justices. The President appoints the justices. Then the justices must be approved by Congress. The justices are appointed for life.

Duties of the Supreme Court
- makes sure that federal, state, and local laws follow the Constitution
- explains the meaning of the Constitution
- decides how to apply the Constitution in specific cases

system of checks and balances
The system that keeps the different branches of government from getting too powerful.

bill
An idea for a law that is presented to Congress.

veto
The power of a President to reject a bill.

The separation of powers keeps each branch of the government from becoming too powerful. Each branch balances the other two and keeps them under control by checking on what they do. This is called the **system of checks and balances**. An example of this system is when the President sends a **bill** to Congress. Congress can decide not to make the bill a law. On the other hand, the President can refuse to approve a bill that Congress has passed. If the President does not agree, he or she can **veto** the bill. Finally, the Supreme Court can decide that a law is unconstitutional. Congress then has the power to rewrite the law.

The Supreme Court, part of the judicial branch, makes sure that laws are constitutional.

> ## Practice

Vocabulary in Context ◆ **Write the word that best completes each sentence.**

1. The Congress is made up of two houses called the

   _____ and the House of Representatives.

2. The President has the power to _____ bills passed by Congress.

3. The courts make up the _____ branch of our government.

census
judicial
Senate
veto

Understanding Time Order ◆ **Choose the words that answer each question. Fill in the circle for your answer.**

4. When does the House of Representatives decide how many representatives can be sent from each state?

   Ⓐ before the census is taken
   Ⓑ after the census is taken
   Ⓒ while they are working on the census
   Ⓓ every two years when they are elected

5. When do the Supreme Court justices need to be approved by Congress?

   Ⓐ before the President appoints them
   Ⓑ after the President appoints them
   Ⓒ after they serve for a year
   Ⓓ both A and C

Drawing Conclusions ◆ **Read the question. Write your answer.**

6. Why do the Congress and the President need to work together to get bills passed?

   _____

   _____

   _____

Strategies for SUCCESS

Cause and Effect

When you study political science, you need to know the causes and effects of certain events. One thing happened. Then a second thing happened as a result. Each sentence below shows cause and effect.

- Because it was well planned, the meeting went smoothly.
- He asked me to do it, so I did.

❖**STRATEGY: Reread the material for clues. Then think.**

1. Watch for the key words that show cause and effect: *so, therefore, as a result, because, make, result, cause, effect, reason, if, since,* and *why.*

2. Ask this question: Did the first thing really cause the second thing to happen?

Part of the Constitution

Exercise 1: Join these two sentences. Use one of these key words to show cause and effect: *because, as a result, so, or therefore.*

The Constitution was carefully written.

It is still a useful plan of government today.

_____

_____

_____

Exercise 2: Read the paragraph below. Circle the key word that helps you see cause and effect.

Some people were afraid that the federal government might be given too much power. So the writers of the Constitution split the federal government into three branches.

The key word *so* helps you see a cause-and-effect relationship between the first and second sentences.

Exercise 3: Rewrite the paragraph on page 100. Change the word *so* to one of these: *As a result, Therefore,* or *Consequently*.

_____

_____

_____

_____

_____

Exercise 4: Do the following sentences show cause and effect? Write *yes* or *no*.

1. Because no one wanted one branch of the federal government to have too much control, a system of checks and balances was developed. _____

2. No one wanted one branch of the federal government to have too much control. As a result, a system of checks and balances was developed. _____

EXECUTIVE

LEGISLATIVE **JUDICIAL**

Exercise 5: Write about an event that happened today. Then write the result of the event or action. Using a key word, join the sentences to show cause and effect.

1. (event or action)

_____

2. (result)

_____

3. _____

_____

State and Local Government

Under the Constitution, the laws of the federal government are stronger than the laws of the states. Only the federal government can print money and set up post offices. The states still have many powers, though. Only the states can grant driver licenses and birth certificates. The federal government and the states share some powers. Both can collect taxes, for example.

Each state has a constitution. The constitutions of most states are modeled after the U.S. Constitution. They all have a Bill of Rights which guarantees basic freedoms.

Like the U.S. government, the governments of all the states have three parts. Each state has a legislative branch to make laws. Each state has an executive branch to carry out laws. Each state also has a judicial branch, a system of courts to interpret laws.

There are differences among state governments. For example, 49 states have two houses in their **legislature**. Nebraska has only one house in its legislature. Some legislatures have only a few dozen members. Others have hundreds. Each state has a different way to decide how many people should be in its legislature. The terms of **legislators** are different lengths of time in different states. Some states limit the number of terms a legislator can be elected to office.

legislature
The branch of government that makes laws.

legislator
A member of a legislature.

Only state governments can grant driver licences.

referendum
A chance for voters to approve or reject laws.

budget
A yearly plan that shows how much money will come in from taxes, fees, and grants and how the money will be spent.

county
The largest division of an American state.

board of supervisors
The government of a county.

States have the same system for making laws as Congress. Sometimes voters can vote on laws by voting in a **referendum**. State legislatures have to vote on proposed changes to the United States Constitution. Congress can suggest amendments, but three-quarters of the state legislatures must agree to them in order for them to become law. Only 27 amendments have been passed in more than two hundred years.

The chief executive of a state is the governor. The power of the governor, like the power of the President, is controlled by the other two branches. One of the most important jobs of the governor is preparing the state **budget**, a plan for raising and spending money.

Every state has courts to rule on state laws about how people and businesses can act. Each state decides how to set up its courts and choose its judges.

A **county** is a division of a state. Most states are divided into counties. There are more than three thousand counties in the United States.

Most counties have their own government elected by the people of the county. This government can be called a county commission, a county legislature, or a **board of supervisors**. The job of this government is to make county

A state Supreme Court ruled that girls should be allowed to play on Little League teams.

laws. A county law is usually called an **ordinance**. Ordinances cover issues like animal, traffic, and noise control. Counties may also have a sheriff and special boards to take care of areas like health or voter registration.

In most states, a county has towns, cities, and villages in it. Some cities, like San Francisco, California, and Denver, Colorado, are not part of a county.

Cities also have legislatures. A city legislature is called a **city council**. Unlike state or national legislatures, city councils usually have only one house. Many American cities have a mayor who heads the city.

Two other types of government are now used in many cities and towns. One type is a **commission**. Three to five elected commissioners are the lawmakers for the town or city. Each commissioner also runs one department of the town or city government. Another type of local government is the council-manager plan. Under this plan, city voters elect a council. The council chooses a manager. The manager works for the council.

Laws made by the national government affect all areas. Laws made by state or local government affect smaller areas.

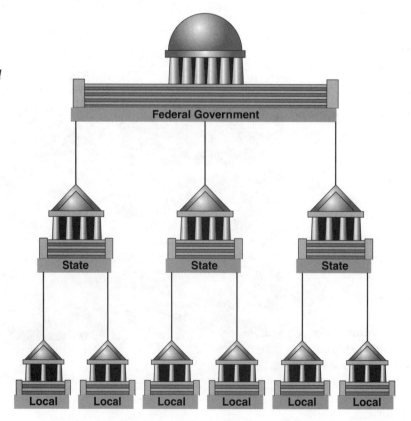

Practice

Vocabulary in Context ◆ **Write the word that best completes each sentence.**

1. After the governor prepares the _____ , the state legislature votes on it.

2. A _____ gives voters a chance to decide if they want to limit the number of terms the governor can serve.

3. Some cities have an _____ against walking a dog without a leash.

4. A _____ is a type of city government.

> budget
> commission
> county
> ordinance
> referendum

Drawing Conclusions ◆ **Write your answer.**

5. Why are state laws more powerful than the laws of a county or city?

_____

_____

Cause and Effect ◆ **Write the word or words that best complete each sentence. Use one of these words: *if, therefore, since,* or *because*.**

6. Only the federal government can print money _____

trade between states would be very difficult _____ each state had its own type of money.

7. The constitutions of Massachusetts and New Hampshire were

written before the United States constitution. _____ those constitutions are not modeled on the U.S. Constitution.

8. _____ each state wrote its own constitution, the number of people in each state legislature and the length of their terms is different.

Check your answers on page 167.

Electing the President

candidate
A person who seeks to be elected to office.

primary
An election where voters choose a candidate.

convention
A meeting at which members of a political party choose their candidates.

poll
A place where people vote.

electoral college
A special group of voters from each state that elects the President and Vice-president.

electors
Members of the electoral college.

Most presidential **candidates** belong to a political party. The two main political parties in the United States are the Democratic Party and the Republican Party. Voters often belong to a political party, too.

There are two kinds of elections: **primary** and general elections. In a primary, only voters who belong to a political party choose the candidate to represent their party. Some states choose candidates with a caucus. In a caucus, members of a political party vote for representatives who attend meetings to choose the party's candidate. In primaries and caucuses, people can vote only for candidates from their party. In general elections, voters can choose any candidate.

Presidential elections take place every four years. In the summer before a presidential election, each political party holds a huge **convention**. Voters from each state send delegates to these conventions. The delegates vote for a presidential candidate from their party. They also vote for a vice-presidential candidate. The first woman chosen as a vice-presidential candidate by a major political party was Geraldine Ferraro. She was chosen by the Democrats in 1984.

Geraldine Ferraro

Election Day for national elections is the first Tuesday in November. Voters go to the **polls** to vote for the President, Vice-president, and other government positions open that year. In most elections, the winner is the candidate who gets the most votes. This kind of election is called direct election. The President and Vice-president, however, are elected by the **electoral college**. The electoral college is made up of **electors** from each state and the District of Columbia.

The number of electors from each state depends on how many people live in that state. Every elector votes for the candidate who received the most votes in that elector's home state. For example, California has 54 electors in the electoral college. The candidate who gets the most votes from the people in California wins the votes of all 54 of California's electors.

A person can be elected President only twice. This limit of two **terms** is the result of an amendment to the Constitution passed in 1951. Another amendment allows the Vice-President to act as President if the President dies, resigns, or is not capable of serving as President.

term
The period of time for which a person holds office.

◆ Extension

Your Right to Vote

For much of the history of this country, not everyone was allowed to vote. African-American men were denied the right to vote until 1870 when the Fifteenth Amendment to the Constitution declared that no one could be denied the right to vote because of race. Although women could vote in some local and state elections, women could not vote in national elections until 1920, when the Nineteenth Amendment declared that no one could be denied the right to vote because of gender.

The Voting Rights Acts of 1965 removed other barriers to voting by African Americans. Though changes in the law allow more people to vote, many do not take advantage of this right. In the 1992 presidential election, only 55 percent of Americans voted.

Do you think it is important to vote? Why or why not? Write your opinion.

_____

_____

Before an election, many newspapers have political cartoons about the candidates. A political cartoon is a drawing that gives an opinion about politics or current events. Political cartoons use **symbols** to show things in the news. Political cartoons use elephants to stand for the Republicans and donkeys to stand for the Democrats. Cartoonists also use other symbols. Doves stand for peace, and bombs stand for weapons. A globe stands for the world as a whole. Cartoons may also use an "Uncle Sam" figure or a bald eagle to stand for the United States. Other countries have symbols, too. A bear often represents Russia, and the Eiffel Tower represents France.

To understand a political cartoon:
- Decide what the figures and objects stand for.
- Look at what the figures are doing.
- Read any words in the cartoon or the title.
- Decide what the cartoonist thinks of the figures and their actions.

In the cartoon on the left, the donkey and the elephant are playing a game. The game they are playing stands for politics. You can read enough of the board to see that the game is Monopoly™. A monopoly is complete control of a business or an industry. This cartoon is a comment on the struggle for power between the two main American political parties.

Practice

Vocabulary in Context ◆ Write the word or words that best complete each sentence.

1. Voters from each party choose the _____

   for their party in a _____ election.

2. An amendment to the Constitution limits to two the number

   of _____ the President can serve.

3. Political cartoons use _____ to stand for things in the news.

candidate
convention
primary
symbols
terms

Understanding Time Order ◆ Choose the words that best answer the question. Fill in the circle for your answer.

4. Which of the following is the first step in electing a president?

   Ⓐ People vote in a general election.
   Ⓑ People vote in a primary election.
   Ⓒ Political conventions are held.
   Ⓓ The legislature meets to vote.

Drawing Conclusions ◆ Choose the words that best complete each sentence. Fill in the circle for your answer.

5. A presidential candidate who wanted to win would probably spend more time campaigning in states with

   Ⓐ many natural resources.
   Ⓑ the most voters.
   Ⓒ the most historic buildings.
   Ⓓ high rates of unemployment.

6. Political cartoons are usually about

   Ⓐ current events.
   Ⓑ events from past history.
   Ⓒ animals.
   Ⓓ the president.

Strategies for SUCCESS

Facts and Opinions

When you study political science, you need to know the difference between facts and opinions. To decide which opinions you agree with, look at the facts that writers or speakers use to back up their opinions. Read the example below.

- The two main political parties in the United States are the Democratic Party and the Republican Party.
- The time has come to form a third political party.

The first example above is a fact. It can be proven. The second sentence is an opinion. Some people may agree with this idea. Others may disagree.

❖**STRATEGY: Think it through.**

1. Look for facts.

2. Look for opinions. Watch for key words that show a statement is an opinion, such as: *I think*, *I believe*, *must*, and *should*. Also look for statements that make a judgment.

3. Ask yourself: Do the facts support the opinions?

Exercise 1: Put an *F* for fact or an *O* for opinion next to each statement.

_____ **1.** U.S. Presidential elections take place every four years.

_____ **2.** In the United States, Election Day is the first Tuesday in November.

_____ **3.** Many other countries hold elections on weekends.

_____ **4.** More Americans would vote if elections were held on Sundays.

_____ **5.** In 1951, an amendment to the Constitution limited the number of times a person can serve as President to two terms.

_____ **6.** There ought to be limits on the number of terms for all elected officials.

_____ **7.** If people want to limit the number of terms an official can serve, they should vote for someone else.

Exercise 2: What opinion is expressed in the following paragraph? What facts are used to support this opinion?

The Electoral College elects the President and Vice-president. There have been three times in United States history when this has not happened, however. The candidates who won the most votes from the people in 1824, 1876, and 1888 did not become President. The Electoral College did not choose the same candidate the people had chosen. The Electoral College is not democratic. Congress has tried to get rid of it several times.

Voting is a right and also a duty.

Opinion: _____

_____

Facts: _____

_____

Exercise 3: Write two facts from this lesson. Add an opinion of your own about the facts you have chosen.

Fact 1: _____

_____

Fact 2: _____

_____

Opinion: _____

From Bills to Laws

New federal laws must be approved by Congress. Only Congress can pass federal laws. The idea for a law is called a bill. Bills can come from several places. Many bills come from members of Congress. Ideas for bills also can come from the President. Sometimes the voters in a state write to their representatives in Congress to suggest ideas for new laws. If a representative agrees with a voter's ideas, he or she will write them up in a proper legal form. Then the representative **sponsors** the bill.

Most bills can be introduced in either the Senate or the House of Representatives. However, bills for raising taxes or other money must be introduced in the House.

When a bill is introduced, it is given a number. Then it is studied by the appropriate **standing committee**. There are committees on special topics like foreign relations, finance, agriculture, and labor.

The committee decides what to do with the bill. There might be a **public hearing** to find out what people think of the bill. The bill might be **tabled** and discussed later. Many bills are rejected by the standing committees.

sponsor
To present a bill and take responsibility for it.

standing committee
A group of senators or representatives who deal with a special topic such as agriculture or foreign relations.

public hearing
A meeting where members of the public are invited to give their opinion.

table
To set aside debate on a bill for a while.

A standing committee of Congress in session

debate
To discuss something from different points of view.

conference committee
A special group of five members from each house that recommends the final form of a bill.

If a bill is not tabled or rejected, it is **debated** and then voted on. If the bill passes in the House of Representatives, it must go to the Senate. Likewise, if it passes in the Senate, it must go to the House for approval. If one house makes changes to a bill, the other house must agree to the changes. More than half of the members of each house of Congress must approve of a bill for it to pass.

If the House of Representatives and the Senate cannot agree on the final form of a bill, they set up a **conference committee**. The conference committee has five members from each house of Congress. Their meetings are private. If the conference committee recommendation is accepted by both houses, the head of each house must sign it. The bill is then sent to the President. If the President signs the bill, it becomes law. The President can also veto the bill. A vetoed bill can still become law if two-thirds or more of the members of each house approve it.

Approximately 10,000 bills are introduced in Congress every year. Only about 100 of these become laws. The laws can be changed by Congress or the Supreme Court. Congress changes laws by the same process used to make the laws. The Supreme Court has the power to remove a law. A law may be challenged in a case that goes to the Supreme Court. Then, the Supreme Court decides if the law is in agreement with the Constitution. If the Supreme Court decides that a law is not constitutional, the law can no longer be enforced.

President Clinton signs legislation implementing the North American Free Trade Agreement.

Lesson 21

How a Bill Becomes Law

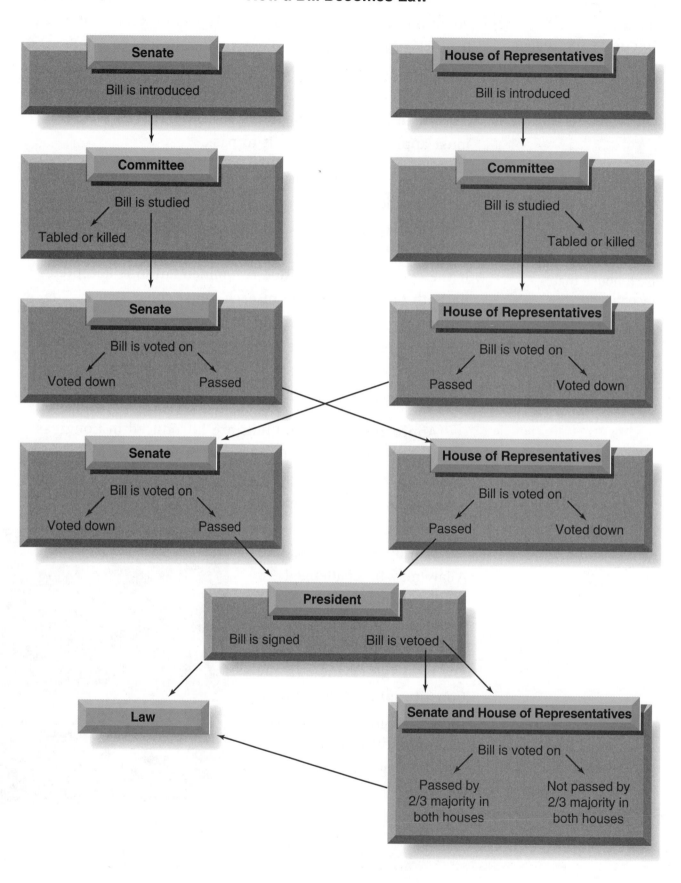

Practice

Vocabulary in Context ◆ **Write the word that best completes each sentence.**

conference
debate
sponsor
standing

1. The Senator or Representative who puts a bill into a proper legal form and takes responsibility for it is

   the _____ of the bill.

2. After the bill gets a number, it goes to a _____ committee that deals with a special topic such as foreign relations or finance.

3. Before Senators or Representatives vote on a bill, they

   _____ it to discuss its good points

   and bad points.

Facts and Opinions ◆ **Put an *F* for fact or an *O* for opinion next to each statement.**

_____ **4.** Before a bill can become a law, it must be voted on by both houses of Congress.

_____ **5.** Congress doesn't get much done because it takes so long to make a bill into a law.

_____ **6.** By making bills pass through so many stages before they can become laws, many bad laws are avoided.

_____ **7.** If the President approves a bill and signs it, it becomes a law.

Understanding Time Order ◆ **Choose the words that best complete the sentence. Fill in the circle for your answer.**

8. A bill is introduced and passed in the House of Representatives. Then the bill

   Ⓐ goes to the Senate.

   Ⓑ goes to a conference committee.

   Ⓒ goes to a standing committee.

   Ⓓ goes to the President.

Check your answers on page 168.

Civil Rights

democracy
Government by the people of a country, either directly or through their elected representatives.

minority
The smaller of two groups.

petition
A formal request, usually written.

Dr. Martin Luther King, Jr., helped organize African Americans in nonviolent demonstrations.

civil rights
The basic rights which every citizen is entitled to.

A **democracy** is a government run by the people, either directly or through their elected representatives. Since everyone will not agree on a position or the best candidate to elect, a democracy is based on the votes of the majority. People who are in the **minority** and vote for the losing candidate or position also have rights which are protected by the U.S. Constitution.

The First Amendment gives all people the right to speak freely. Also, the government cannot prevent a person from printing the truth, even if he or she is critical of the government. The government may not set up an official religion or keep people from choosing their own religion and practicing it freely.

The First Amendment also protects people's right to form groups. People can try to change the government by holding demonstrations or starting **petitions**. Peaceful demonstrations and petitions are ways to get the government's attention when people want changes.

The Constitution and its Amendments were designed to protect the rights of everyone. Yet, under this Constitution, many African Americans were slaves. They did not have the same rights that other Americans enjoyed. They could not vote, so they could not help elect people who would work to end slavery. It was not until 1865 that the Thirteenth Amendment ended slavery. In 1868, the Fourteenth Amendment declared that all African Americans were citizens of the United States. They were entitled to the same protection under the law as any other citizen. Finally, in 1870, the Fifteenth Amendment gave African-American men the right to vote.

Even though the Thirteenth, Fourteenth, and Fifteenth Amendments gave more rights to African Americans, these rights were often not applied fairly. The **Civil Rights** Act of 1875 tried to make sure that African Americans were treated equally in public places, such as hotels, railroad stations, and theaters.

discriminating
Treating people in unequal and unfair ways.

segregation
Separating people on the basis of race.

In 1883, the Supreme Court ruled that the federal government could make laws to prevent states from **discriminating** against African Americans. However, it also said that the federal government could not prevent private citizens from banning African Americans from their businesses. This decision was a major setback for African Americans' struggle for equality. It allowed a system of **segregation** to be applied in almost every situation. Segregation meant that African-American citizens were separated from white citizens on buses and trains, in schools and hospitals, on the job, and in restaurants.

Civil rights groups were first formed in the beginning of the 20th century, but little changed. The civil rights groups needed a new plan. Instead of waiting for the laws to change, these groups took action into their own hands. Beginning in the 1950s, Dr. Martin Luther King, Jr., and other religious leaders helped to organize people in non-violent demonstrations and gave public speeches in support of increased civil rights for African Americans.

In 1957, Federal troops were sent to make sure states obeyed new laws against segregation.

The process of changing the law to extend equal rights to all citizens has been a long one. In 1954, the Supreme Court passed a historic decision in the case of *Brown v. the Board of Education of Topeka, Kansas.* In this case, the Supreme Court decided that public education could not be segregated. The court ordered that public schools must stop segregating students. In 1955, in Montgomery, Alabama, African Americans challenged the local laws and refused to sit in the back of buses. Then they boycotted the Montgomery bus system. This forced the bus system to change its **policy**.

In 1964, the Civil Rights Act was passed. This protected the voting rights of all citizens and made segregation illegal. The federal government now had the power to punish anyone who practiced discrimination. It could also cut off money to the states that didn't obey the law.

Other groups also began to ask for equal rights. People with physical disabilities learned from the struggle of African Americans. In the 1960s, groups of disabled people and those who cared about them began a campaign. In the 1970s, Congress passed laws requiring public schools to accept students with disabilities.

In 1990, Congress passed the Americans with Disabilities Act. This law says that public places—including restaurants, theaters, and stores—must be accessible to disabled people. There must be parking places for handicapped people. Ramps or elevators are needed for people in wheelchairs. Restrooms must be designed for use by a person in a wheelchair. An employer cannot refuse to hire people just because they are disabled.

Not all groups working for their civil rights are successful, however. The Equal Rights Amendment was passed by Congress in 1972. Its goal was to ban all discrimination against women because of their gender. By 1982, it had not been ratified by enough states, so the amendment was not added to the constitution.

policy
The way a business is managed; the rules of a business.

A public school kindergarten

Practice

Vocabulary in Context ◆ Write the word that best completes each sentence.

1. A group campaigning for wheelchair ramps at the shopping center was asking shoppers to sign their

   _____ .

2. Public schools had to admit students of all races after

   the Supreme Court ruled that _____
   was not allowed.

3. Many businesses find it a good _____
   to help employees get their GED.

democracy
petition
policy
segregation

Cause and Effect ◆ Choose the words that best complete the sentence. Fill in the circle for your answer.

4. All African Americans became citizens as a result of

   Ⓐ the Supreme Court reversing the Civil Rights Act of 1875.
   Ⓑ the Fourteenth Amendment to the Constitution.
   Ⓒ the Fifteenth Amendment to the Constitution.
   Ⓓ the African-American boycott of the Alabama bus system.

Facts and Opinions ◆ Put an *F* for fact or an *O* for opinion next to each statement.

_____ 5. According to the Supreme Court, segregation must not be practiced.

_____ 6. People generally prefer to spend time with others who are like themselves.

_____ 7. It is a shame that the Equal Rights Amendment was not approved to be part of the Constitution.

Check your answers on page 168.

Thinking and Writing

1. Many of the founders of the United States had lived under the rule of a king or queen. They did not believe any one person should have so much power. How does the Constitution make sure that no single person in government gets too much power?

_____

_____

_____

_____

2. Most Americans agree that the most important rights are the right to vote, the right to free speech, the right to choose their own religion, and the right to a fair trial when they are accused of breaking a law. Which right is most important to you?

_____

_____

_____

_____

3. Many people believe that in a democracy, like the United States, citizens have a duty to be well-informed. How do you get information about current events? How does what you know about current events affect the way you vote?

_____

_____

_____

_____

Check your answers on pages 168–169.

Unit 5

BEHAVIORAL SCIENCE

What do you know about behavior?
Write something you know about it.

_____

_____

Preview the unit by looking at the titles and pictures. **Write something that you predict you will learn about behavior.**

_____

_____

When you study behavior, you learn why people act and feel as they do. A person's behavior is affected by the world he or she lives in. The study of people's behavior is behavioral science.

In this unit you will learn about:
◆ the physical and social basis of behavior
◆ feelings and mental health
◆ ways to change behavior

The Basis of Behavior

nervous system
The body system made up of the brain, spinal cord, and nerves.

Behavior is controlled by the **nervous system**. Some nerves of the nervous system carry messages to the brain. There, the messages are processed and stored. The brain sends signals through other nerves to the rest of the body.

When you smell food, nerves in the nose carry messages to your brain. There, the messages are processed and the odors are identified. Then, the brain sends signals to different parts of your body. Your mouth may water and your stomach may growl. You may feel hungry. You may respond to these feelings by eating. All of these actions happen because of the nervous system.

hormones
Natural chemicals in the body. When released into the bloodstream they affect body organs.

Hormones can also affect behavior. One type of hormone, adrenaline, is related to fear. Imagine that you are walking along a road. Suddenly you see a car start to skid. It's headed toward you! As you see the car skid, adrenaline is released into your blood stream. It makes your heart beat faster and your breathing rate go up. The release of this hormone helps you run out of the path of the car. Adrenaline can be released because of an imaginary scare. For example, adrenaline makes your heart pound when you watch a frightening movie.

socialization
The process of learning the rules of behavior of a social group.

Behavior can also be learned. One way of learning behavior is through **socialization**. Socialization helps a person fit into a social group. Social groups include families, workplaces, churches, and clubs.

norm
The ideas and informal rules shared by the members of a social group.

There are rules of behavior in every social group. These rules are called **norms**. For instance, wearing a suit is the norm for many people who work in banks and offices. Every social group also has **values**. Values tell a person what a social group considers to be good or right. Some examples of values are honesty, fair play, and hard work.

values
The ideas that a society considers to be most important.

role
An expected way
of behaving.

*Parents can model
behaviors they want
their children to learn.*

model
To set an example.

culture
The beliefs and ways
of doing things in a
society.

body language
A way of communi-
cating feelings without
speaking, for example,
by using the face or
moving the body.

Norms and values are not the same. Norms are based on values. Still, values are usually more important than norms. For example, a person may think that it is important to go to work. This is a value. However, this person may not think that the norm of dressing up for work is important.

Socialization prepares a person for a **role** in society. Boys are usually socialized to become fathers someday. Fathers are expected to help support their families. Most fathers are also expected to know about cars, tools, and machines. Roles in society can change. Then socialization for those roles changes, too.

There are other ways that people learn behaviors. For example, people can learn from the environment. A child who touches a hot stove learns to avoid hot stoves. Something in the environment has helped the child learn a new behavior.

Another way to learn behavior is by watching others. For example, parents can **model** behavior for their children. If parents read to their children, the children may start to read on their own. Parents can also model behaviors like throwing a baseball or changing a tire. Parents can also model values like fair play and sharing.

A person's **culture** can also affect behavior. Culture is a social group's beliefs and ways of doing things. There are differences in cultural beliefs. For instance, some groups have different beliefs about personal space. People from South America may stand close to each other while talking. People from Western countries may prefer to stand farther apart. Another difference in cultures is in the use of **body language**. People from Japan may bow to show respect to another person. People from the United States may stand up to show respect.

Practice

Vocabulary in Context ◆ **Write the word that best completes each sentence.**

1. _____ are natural body chemicals that can affect behavior.

2. People learn to become members of social groups through

   _____ .

3. Respecting older people is a _____ in many cultures.

hormones

role

socialization

value

Drawing Conclusions ◆ **Choose the words that best answer each question. Fill in the circle for your answer.**

4. Which of the following is an example of a parent's role?

   Ⓐ getting plenty of exercise

   Ⓑ volunteering at a day-care center

   Ⓒ making sure young family members attend school

   Ⓓ running for public office

5. When you become angry, your heart beats faster because of

   Ⓐ socialization.

   Ⓑ adrenaline.

   Ⓒ culture.

   Ⓓ both A and B

Cause and Effect ◆ **Write the words that best complete the sentence. Fill in the circle for your answer.**

6. If a child is not socialized, the child

   Ⓐ will never learn to play group sports.

   Ⓑ may never attend college.

   Ⓒ may not be invited to many birthday parties.

   Ⓓ will not learn the norms and the values of society.

Check your answers on page 169.

The Changing Family

family
A social group made up of people who are part of one household and are usually related to each other.

There are many kinds of **families**. The nuclear family is made up of two parents and one or more children. The single-parent family is one of the fastest growing family types. It is made up of one parent and one or more children. Most single-parent families are headed by women.

Another kind of family is the blended family. When two divorced people marry again, they often bring children from their former marriages. They may also have children together. This creates a blended family.

The extended family is common in some cultures. It is made up of parents, their children, and other relatives who live in the same home. Grandparents, aunts, uncles, or cousins may be part of an extended family.

Foster families are temporary families for some children. Often the courts will place a child who has had problems at home in foster care. The child lives with a foster family until the child can be adopted. Some children in foster care are returned to their parents.

There are other, less common, types of families. Some families are made up of two people who are not married.

communal
Refers to a group of related and unrelated people who live together and share among themselves.

The couple sometimes raises children together. Some people live in **communal** families. These families may consist of single adults and married couples and their children. Members of the communal family may share chores and expenses.

An extended family may include a couple's children and elderly parents.

Since the 1950s, the American family has been changing. The graph below shows these changes. As you can see, the number of nuclear families has decreased. The number of single-parent families has increased. Experts think that the rise in single-parent families is partly the result of rising divorce rates. It is also the result of a rise in teen pregnancy.

The Changing Family

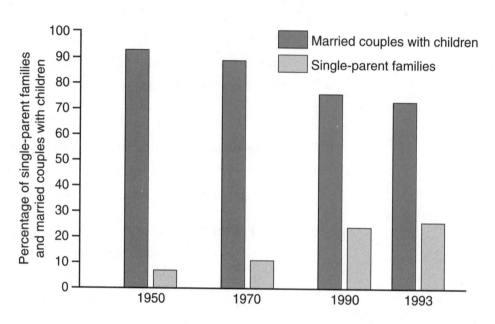

Though it has many forms, the family is still the basic unit of society. One of its main jobs is to take care of family members, especially children. The family provides for basic needs like food, clothing, and shelter. The family also provides emotional support and cares for family members who are ill.

The family is usually the first group in which a child is socialized. It prepares children to be part of other social groups such as schools and neighborhoods. When children are socialized, they **internalize** the values and norms their families have taught them at home. For example, some values that many people agree on are honesty and hard work. Families can teach honesty by urging their children to tell the truth. Families teach the value of work by having their children do chores.

internalize
To personally accept and use the norms and values of a society.

Practice

Vocabulary in Context ◆ Write the word that best completes each sentence.

1. The _____ is usually the first group in which a child is socialized.

2. Children learn to become members of society as they _____ the norms and values of their parents.

3. A _____ family contains related and unrelated people who live together.

> communal
> family
> internalize
> role

Finding Facts ◆ Choose the words that best answer each question. Fill in the circle for your answer.

4. Which of the following is an example of a nuclear family?

   Ⓐ a group of adults who are not related to each other
   Ⓑ a mother, father, three children, and a grandfather
   Ⓒ a mother, father, and five children
   Ⓓ a father and his two children

5. Look at the graph on page 126. Which of the following describes the change in the American family?

   Ⓐ The percentage of single-parent families has grown.
   Ⓑ The percentage of nuclear families has increased.
   Ⓒ The American family has fallen apart.
   Ⓓ More people are starting families.

Cause and Effect ◆ Choose the words that best complete the sentence. Fill in the circle for your answer.

6. If the family cannot perform its role, then

   Ⓐ children may not learn values like honesty.
   Ⓑ the basic needs of family members may not be met.
   Ⓒ family members may not get emotional support.
   Ⓓ all of the above

Check your answers on page 169.

Finding the Main Idea

1. The Topic Sentence

Studying social studies becomes easier if you know how to pick out main ideas. A paragraph often has one sentence that tells the main idea. It is the topic sentence. Read the example below. What is the topic sentence of the paragraph?

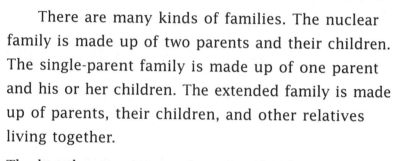

There are many kinds of families. The nuclear family is made up of two parents and their children. The single-parent family is made up of one parent and his or her children. The extended family is made up of parents, their children, and other relatives living together.

The last three sentences give example of types of families. The first sentence ties the examples together. The first sentence is the topic sentence.

> ❖**STRATEGY:** **Find the topic sentence that tells the main idea.**
>
> **1.** Look for the sentence that ties all the other sentences together in the paragraph.
>
> **2.** Remember that the topic sentence can be anywhere in the paragraph. It is usually the first or last sentence.

Exercise 1: **Read the paragraph. Write the topic sentence.**

Foster families are temporary families for some children. Often the courts will place a child who has had problems at home in foster care. The child lives with a foster family until the child can be adopted. Some children in foster care are returned to their parents.

The topic sentence of the paragraph is:

_____

2. The Implied Main Idea

Sometimes a paragraph has no topic sentence. The writer gives hints or examples but does not state the main idea. You have to figure out the main idea yourself. Look at the example below. What is the implied main idea of the paragraph?

> The family is usually the main social group in which a child is socialized. It prepares children to be part of other social groups like schools and neighborhoods. The family also takes care of family members. It provides for basic needs such as food, clothing, and shelter.

The first two sentences of the paragraph deal with the family's role in socializing children. The other sentences deal with the family's role in caring for its members. The main idea is that the role of the family includes many functions.

❖**STRATEGY: Find the implied main idea.**

1. Ask yourself: How do all the sentences relate to each other? What is the writer hinting?

2. Use what you know to figure out the main idea.

Exercise 2: Read the paragraph below. Write the main idea.

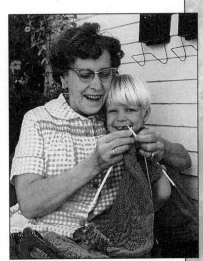

> One kind of family is the nuclear family. It is made up of two parents and one or more children. The single-parent family is made up of one parent and one or more children. The extended family is larger. It is made up of parents, children, and other relatives who live in the same home. The blended family forms when two divorced people marry again. The two parents bring children from their former marriages.

The main idea of the paragraph is:

_____

How People Handle Feelings

Feelings help people relate to and care for one another. Feelings also help people survive. For example, a father or mother could not properly care for a child if he or she did not have feelings of love for the child. Without loving care, a child may not survive.

People have a wide range of feelings. Most feelings are normal. Anger, fear, and hate are just as normal as love and happiness. Still, some feelings can get out of control. For example, some people act out their anger by throwing things, or by hitting objects or other people. These behaviors are usually harmful.

Some people become angry more easily than others. Such people are said to have a "quick temper." However, people who become angry easily can learn to deal with their anger. A helpful hint for an angry person is to "count to ten" before saying or doing something about the situation. A person who has taken time to calm down will do a better job solving the problem.

Anger isn't the only normal feeling that can go too far. Most people feel sad at times. This is normal. A person may feel sad after the breakup of a romance. When a loved one dies, a person may have feelings of **grief**.

grief
Deep sadness.

People's emotions often show on their faces.

However, sadness that lasts a very long time or that is extreme is not normal. A person who feels this way may suffer from **depression**. This person may feel that life has no meaning. People who are depressed often feel that they have no hope.

Severe depression is a serious problem. It can cause great suffering. A depressed person may need help from a doctor. Some depressed people need treatment in a hospital. With help, many depressed people get better.

There are other mental and emotional disorders that may need treatment. One type of disorder causes people to lose touch with reality. Such people may hear voices or see visions that are not there. They may also feel that someone is trying to harm them.

Another disorder involves extreme fear. Such fears are called **phobias**. For example, some people fear being in public places. They may panic if they have to leave their homes. This type of phobia makes it hard for the person to function in society.

Most people do not have emotional or mental disorders. Still, everyone must learn to cope with the everyday problems of life. One common problem that most people deal with is **stress**. Though stress is normal, too much stress can lead to emotional problems like depression. Stress can also lead to physical problems like high blood pressure or stomach upset.

depression
An emotional disorder marked by extreme or prolonged sadness.

phobia
An unfounded or extreme fear.

A person who has a fear of public places may have trouble shopping at a mall.

stress
Emotional tension.

There are many signs of stress. Some of them are headaches, sweaty palms, and rapid breathing. The person under stress may not be able to sleep at night. Other signs include shaking or nervous twitches. Some people become moody, angry, or depressed. Sometimes people cope with stress in harmful ways. They may drink alcohol or eat too much food. They may also take their feelings out on others.

To cope with stress, doctors suggest exercising and eating healthful foods. Talking about problems with another person also helps reduce stress. Taking time for fun activities like seeing a movie or visiting a friend may reduce stress. Some people also find that humor helps reduce stress.

Extension

How do you cope with stress?

People may feel stress on their jobs. Family problems may be stressful. Even happy events such as weddings, parties, or graduations may cause stress.

Think about your activities over the past week. What situations caused you stress? Think about ways you might cope with stress.

List three situations that caused you stress. Then write ways to cope with stress.

Situations:

_____

_____

_____

Ways to Cope:

_____

_____

_____

Check your answers on page 169.

Practice

Vocabulary in Context ◆ **Write the word that best completes each sentence.**

1. A person who is very sad and feels that life is hopeless

   may suffer from _____ .

2. A person who is terrified of heights may have a

   _____ .

3. Sometimes exercise can help reduce _____ .

depression
emotions
phobia
stress

Finding Facts ◆ **Choose the words that best answer each question. Fill in the circle for your answer.**

4. Why is too much stress harmful?

   Ⓐ It can lead to harmful behaviors like eating too much.

   Ⓑ It can lead to high blood pressure.

   Ⓒ It can lead to emotional problems like depression.

   Ⓓ all of the above

5. Which problem is most likely to need treatment by a doctor?

   Ⓐ anger

   Ⓑ grief

   Ⓒ depression

   Ⓓ stress

Finding the Main Idea ◆ **Choose the words that best answer the question. Fill in the circle for your answer.**

6. Which sentence best summarizes the first paragraph on page 132?

   Ⓐ Stress makes a person unable to sleep.

   Ⓑ Stress causes some people to have headaches.

   Ⓒ There are many signs of stress.

   Ⓓ Stress causes some people to become moody.

Check your answers on pages 169–170.

Summarizing

A summary is a brief statement of the main ideas and facts in a passage. Writing a summary can help you understand and remember what you read. Read the example below. Then study the summary of the passage.

People have a wide range of feelings. Most feelings are normal. Anger, fear, and hate are just as normal as love and happiness. Still, some feelings can get out of control. For example, some people act out their anger by throwing things, or by hitting objects or other people. These behaviors are often harmful.

Summary: People have many different feelings, most of which are normal. However, some feelings can get out of control.

❖**STRATEGY: Think about the ideas in the passage.**

1. Read the passage and list the most important facts.

2. Find the main idea.

3. In your own words, summarize the passage.

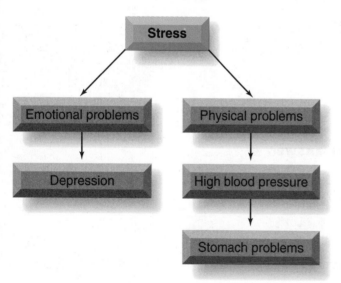

Exercise 1: Read the passage. Then answer the questions.

Everyone must learn to cope with the everyday problems of life. One common problem that most people deal with is stress. Though stress is normal, too much stress can lead to emotional problems like depression. Stress can also lead to stomach problems or high blood pressure.

1. Write the topic, main idea, and most important facts.

Topic: _____

Main Idea: _____

_____

Important Facts: _____

_____

2. Write a summary of the passage.

_____

_____

_____

_____

_____

Exercise 2: Read the passage below. Write two or three sentences that summarize the passage.

Another disorder involves extreme fear. Such fears are called **phobias**. For example, some people fear being in public places. They may panic if they have to leave their homes. This type of phobia makes it hard for the person to function in society.

Summary:

_____

_____

_____

_____

_____

Counselors can help people overcome phobias.

Check your answers on page 170.

Behavioral Psychology

Scientists who study behavior are called behavioral psychologists. They study the ways people and animals respond to the world they live in. Behavioral psychologists usually study behavior in planned experiments. They can control a person's or animal's **environment**. Then they see how that person or animal reacts. Behavioral psychologists are more interested in what their **subjects** do than in what their feelings and thoughts are.

Behavioral psychologists often do experiments with animals, such as monkeys and rats. Such experiments help behavioral psychologists understand human behavior. B.F. Skinner was one of the first behavioral psychologists. He did many experiments with animals, especially pigeons. He studied the pigeon's random behavior of pecking food. He changed the **random** behavior into a specific behavior. Skinner used **reinforcement** techniques to do this.

At first, Skinner fed the pigeon when it pecked at anything. Then he fed the pigeon when it pecked on the wall near a lever. Then, when the pigeon pecked the lever, a door opened and more food appeared. The pigeon **associated** pecking the lever with getting fed. The food was a reward for the correct behavior. Rewarding correct behavior is called positive reinforcement.

Other scientists have used **punishment** to teach animals. For example, a rat was taught how to run through a maze. Every time the rat made a wrong turn, it got an electric shock through the metal floor. The rat remembered the shocks. It learned to make the turns that did not cause it to be shocked.

The pigeon learned how to peck at the lever through good experiences. The rat learned to run through the maze correctly through bad experiences. Children learn how to behave through good and bad experiences, too. For example, we use positive reinforcement, such as praise, when children

environment
Everything that surrounds an animal or person.

subject
The animal or person that is being studied in an experiment.

random
Having no particular order or pattern.

reinforcement
A way to encourage a type of behavior.

associate
To connect two ideas or events in one's mind.

punishment
A way to discourage a type of behavior.

modify
To change.

behave the way we want them to. We use punishment, such as scolding, when they behave in a way we don't want them to. Each time we do this, we are trying to **modify** the children's behavior.

Some experts think that positive reinforcement works better than punishment. Positive reinforcement focuses on what a person does right, not what he or she does wrong. For example, a parent might praise a child for being polite. The praise shows the child that politeness is valued. Scolding the child for being rude only teaches the child what not to do. Scolding may not teach the child how to be polite. It also may not show that politeness is important.

Positive reinforcement also can be used on the job. Many employers praise their workers for doing a good job. Merit raises and bonuses are positive reinforcers. They encourage workers to meet certain goals. For example, a worker might get a bonus for bringing in new business.

Some ways of giving positive reinforcement work better than others. For example, some people praise students for getting good grades. Yet, this praise may not reinforce the actions that lead to good grades. Instead, some experts advise praising students for studying.

Positive reinforcement can help shape a child's behavior.

addiction
A need for something that is habit-forming like cigarettes, alcohol, or drugs.

nicotine
The addictive substance in tobacco.

Some programs use behavior modification to help people stop smoking.

Behavioral scientists also study behavioral problems. **Addiction** is a serious behavioral problem. It can lead to harmful actions. For example, people can become addicted to **nicotine**. Many such people keep smoking even though they know that smoking can cause cancer. An alcoholic may drive while drunk even though he or she risks causing an accident.

Types of Addiction

- alcohol
- nicotine
- illegal drugs (cocaine, heroin, etc.)
- prescription drugs (tranquilizers, sleeping pills, etc.)
- behaviors (gambling, overeating, working, etc.)

Some experts think addiction is a disease. They believe that it may have a physical cause. Other experts think that emotional problems like low self-esteem may lead to addiction. Scientists have found that the children of addicts are at risk for becoming addicts. This may mean that addiction is partly inherited.

Behavior modification can be used to help people with addictions. For example, people who smoke can chew gum or hold straws to keep them busy. New hobbies or lots of exercise can also help distract the smoker. Other behavioral changes may include avoiding places where there are smokers or viewing photos of damaged lungs.

Behavioral scientists keep looking for new ways to help people with addictions change their behavior. They hope people will be able to learn ways to avoid addictions. The more scientists know about how people learn, the more they can help people to learn behaviors that are good for them.

Practice

Vocabulary in Context ◆ **Write the word that best completes each sentence.**

1. A person who cannot stop drinking alcohol may have

   an _____ to alcohol.

2. A person's surroundings are his or her _____ .

> addiction
> associate
> environment

Finding the Main Idea ◆ **Choose the words that best answer each question. Fill in the circle for your answer.**

3. What is the main idea of the first paragraph on page 136?

   Ⓐ Behavioral psychologists want to find out what people's feelings are.

   Ⓑ Behavioral psychologists are only interested in animals.

   Ⓒ Behavioral psychologists are interested in the way that people and animals respond to the world they live in.

   Ⓓ all of the above

4. What is the main idea of the first paragraph on page 137?

   Ⓐ We try to modify the children's behavior.

   Ⓑ The pigeon learned how to peck at the lever through a good experience.

   Ⓒ Positive reinforcement and punishment can be used to modify behavior.

   Ⓓ Children should be scolded and praised.

Summarizing ◆ **Choose the words that best answer the question. Fill in the circle for your answer.**

5. Which sentence best summarizes the last two paragraphs on page 137?

   Ⓐ Workers can be offered bonuses.

   Ⓑ Praise and rewards are ways of giving positive reinforcement.

   Ⓒ It is better to praise children for studying than for getting good grades.

   Ⓓ Scolding is not a form of positive reinforcement.

Check your answers on page 170.

Social Problems

Over time, societies change. Changes in technology, such as the invention of new machines, may cause some people to lose their jobs. A growing population may cause people to live in crowded conditions. Although changes in society can lead to good things, sometimes these changes also lead to problems. Two such problems are an increase in crime and an increase in the number of people who are **homeless**. Many people think that only cities have these social problems. However, this is not true.

homeless
Without a permanent address.

HOMELESSNESS. There are between 250,000 and one million homeless people in the United States. Many of the homeless are women, children, and families. Some women become homeless after their families break up. The number of homeless families with children is growing faster than any other homeless group.

Many homeless people have finished high school or have gone to college. Many have jobs. Others are laid-off workers who cannot find new jobs. They may not have the right skills for new jobs that are being created. Often they must take **minimum wage** jobs that don't pay enough for them to pay the rent.

minimum wage
The lowest hourly wage allowed to be paid a U.S. worker.

Some homeless people are alcoholics or former mental patients. In the early 1980s, state mental hospitals began releasing large numbers of patients. At that time many doctors thought that keeping people in hospitals for long periods did them little good. It was also costly. However, there were few services to help former mental patients adjust to the world. As a result, many of them ended up living on the streets. Experts think that about a third of homeless people are mentally ill.

Many experts think that homelessness has increased because of changes in public policy. In the early 1980s, many government programs that provided a "safety net" for people

affordable housing
Homes for people with low incomes.

shelter
A temporary dwelling for homeless persons.

People have responded to rising crime by protecting themselves and their neighbors.

with low incomes were cut. For example, programs to provide **affordable housing** were cut from the budget. As the number of people needing housing went up, the number of affordable-housing units went down.

The lack of affordable housing is a major problem in the United States. Some people have to spend as much as 70 percent of their income on housing. People who can't pay the rent lose their homes or apartments. Many of them may then become homeless.

Many communities are trying to help homeless people. Some people donate food and clothing to **shelters**. Others volunteer to work for groups that help homeless families.

CRIME. If you watch the news on TV or read a newspaper, you will probably find an article about a crime. The number of violent crimes in the United States increased by more than 50 percent from 1983 to 1992. People feel afraid. They are afraid to go out at night. They are afraid to let their children play in a nearby park.

People who used to leave doors unlocked are now buying extra-strong locks. Many people have alarms on their homes and their cars. In some places, people say that they feel like prisoners in their homes.

In many communities, people have become tired of hiding from crime. They have started looking for ways to fight crime. People have formed groups to watch for each other. Many police departments have helped people start these "neighborhood watch" programs.

By helping at homeless shelters and taking part in neighborhood watch programs, people are working to make society better. Change can start with one person's idea and then expand to larger groups and neighborhood organizations. Many people are doing their part, however small, in trying to change the social problems that affect everyone.

Practice

Vocabulary in Context ◆ **Write the word that best completes each sentence.**

1. A decrease in _____ housing may cause rising homelessness.

2. Many homeless people live in _____ until they can find a permanent place to live.

affordable

minimum

shelters

Cause and Effect ◆ **Choose the words that best complete each sentence. Fill in the circle for your answer.**

3. State mental hospitals released many patients in the 1980s because

   Ⓐ the patients were ready to re-enter society.
   Ⓑ doctors felt that keeping patients in the hospital for long periods of time did them little good.
   Ⓒ hospitals needed the space for new patients.
   Ⓓ the patients wanted to be released.

4. People may become homeless because

   Ⓐ their families break up.
   Ⓑ they lose their jobs.
   Ⓒ they can't afford their housing bills.
   Ⓓ all of the above

Summarizing ◆ **Choose the words that best answer the question. Fill in the circle for your answer.**

5. Which sentence best summarizes the ideas expressed in the last two paragraphs on 141?

   Ⓐ Many people are active in trying to fight social problems and help make society better.
   Ⓑ Many people are afraid of their neighborhoods.
   Ⓒ Many people want the police to come into their neighborhoods for protection.
   Ⓓ Many people are tired of fighting crime.

Check your answers on page 170.

Thinking and Writing

1. Scientists study the behavior of humans and animals. Why do you think it is important to study behavior?

_____

_____

_____

_____

2. Lesson 23 explained some of the factors behind behavior. Think about a person riding on a roller coaster. Describe some of the things the person might be doing. What are some reasons for these behaviors?

_____

_____

_____

_____

3. In this unit, you read about several different types of families. Describe your family or describe the family of someone you know. What type of family is it?

_____

_____

_____

_____

4. Think about different feelings you may have experienced this week. Choose a pleasant feeling and describe it.

_____

_____

_____

Check your answers on page 170–171.

Check What You've Learned

Check What You've Learned will give you an idea of how well you've learned to understand social studies content using the skills in this book.

You will read paragraphs, maps, charts, and graphs followed by one or more multiple-choice questions. There is a total of 20 questions. There is no time limit.

Read each passage and question carefully. Fill in the circle for the best answer.

Questions 1–2 are based on the following map.

Climates of the Eastern United States

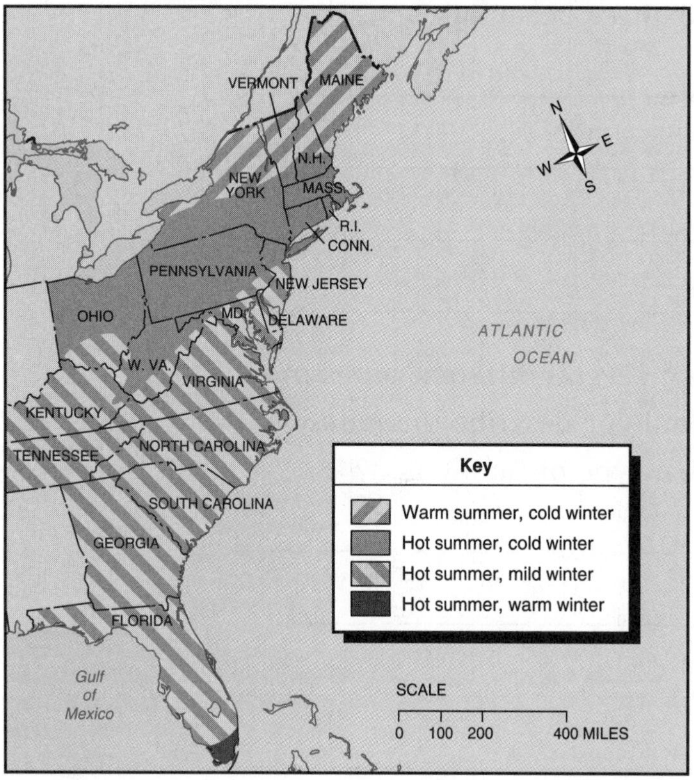

Key

Warm summer, cold winter
Hot summer, cold winter
Hot summer, mild winter
Hot summer, warm winter

SCALE
0   100 200   400 MILES

1. Which state or states has a tropical climate of hot summers and warm winters?
   Ⓐ South Carolina
   Ⓑ Florida
   Ⓒ all the states south of Virginia
   Ⓓ South Carolina and Florida

2. Which of these statements is true based on the information on the map?

Ⓐ Georgia has mild winters and hot summers.

Ⓑ Maine has cold winters and cold summers.

Ⓒ New York state has the most snow.

Ⓓ Three different climate zones can be found in Pennsylvania and New Jersey.

Questions 3–6 are based on the following passage.

Hawaii is the fiftieth state of the Union. It's the only state that isn't on the North American continent. Hawaii is a group of eight islands in the northern Pacific Ocean. The Hawaiian islands were formed by volcanoes.

The economy of Hawaii benefits from good weather, fertile land, and beautiful beaches. The early Hawaiians lived by farming and fishing. The rich soil and warm climate are ideal for crops like sugar cane, coffee, and pineapples. In the late 1880s, Chinese, Japanese, Filipino, and Portuguese laborers went to work on the Hawaiian sugar and pineapple plantations. After World War II, many people moved from the plantations to the cities to work in the tourist industry.

There are people from many different cultures living together in Hawaii. Hawaii is often called the "melting pot of the Pacific." However, the way of life—the government, the language, the way people dress—has been American since 1900. From 1900 to 1959, Hawaii was an American territory. Then it became the fiftieth state.

3. You can conclude that the main language spoken in Hawaii is

Ⓐ Hawaiian.

Ⓑ Chinese.

Ⓒ Filipino.

Ⓓ English.

145

4. Hawaii is ideal for crops like sugar cane because

Ⓐ the land is fertile.

Ⓑ the climate is warm.

Ⓒ the islands were formed by volcanoes.

Ⓓ both A and B

5. Hawaii became an American territory

Ⓐ after it became a state.

Ⓑ in 1959.

Ⓒ in the 1880s.

Ⓓ after 1900.

6. Based on the last paragraph, you could infer that "melting pot" means a place where

Ⓐ different kinds of food are made.

Ⓑ the temperature is very high.

Ⓒ people from different cultures live together.

Ⓓ all of the above

Questions 7–8 are based on the following paragraph.

In the 1800s, the U.S. government wanted people to settle the western part of the country. The Homestead Act was passed in 1862. The Act gave 160 acres of land to anyone who moved out west and worked the land for five years. People began settling Nebraska, the Dakotas, and the Kansas plains. Other people went west during the Gold Rush. In 1874, 15,000 people went to the Dakotas to look for gold.

7. Which of the following statements about the Homestead Act is an opinion?

Ⓐ The Homestead Act was passed in 1862.

Ⓑ The people who went out west under the Homestead Act were braver than those who stayed in the East.

Ⓒ The land given away under the Homestead Act was in Nebraska, the Dakotas, and the Kansas plains.

Ⓓ The Homestead Act gave 160 acres of land to anyone who moved out west and worked the land for five years.

8. The Homestead Act and the Gold Rush are similar because

Ⓐ both were started by the government.

Ⓑ both began in 1874.

Ⓒ both caused people to move west.

Ⓓ neither encouraged people to settle down in the West.

Questions 9–11 are based on the following graph.

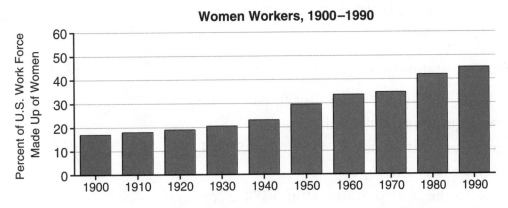

9. The biggest increase in the number of women as a percent of the U.S. work force occurred between

Ⓐ 1910 and 1920.

Ⓑ 1940 and 1950.

Ⓒ 1950 and 1960.

Ⓓ 1980 and 1990.

10. This graph shows

Ⓐ occasional increases in the number of women in the work force, followed by declines.

Ⓑ a general decrease in the number of women in the work force.

Ⓒ a fairly steady number of women in the work force.

Ⓓ a steady increase in the number of women in the work force.

11. You can infer from this graph that

Ⓐ women workers are paid more than men.

Ⓑ most women who work finished high school.

Ⓒ a higher percentage of children born in 1980 have mothers who work than did children born in 1920.

Ⓓ all of the above

In 1870, about one third of the workers in U.S. factories had not been born in the United States. Most of these immigrants had come from countries in western and northern Europe, such as England, Ireland, and Germany. After 1880, people from southern and eastern Europe began to come to the United States to join the work force. The new immigrants were from Hungary, Greece, Italy, Russia, and Poland.

12. Which of the following statements is a fact?

Ⓐ People who came to the United States in the late 1800s were very unhappy in their homelands.

Ⓑ After 1880, people began to come to the United States from southern and eastern Europe.

Ⓒ People who came to the United States after 1880 were hoping to get rich and then go back home.

Ⓓ In 1870, the one third of the workers in U.S. factories who had not been born in the United States were grateful to have jobs.

13. What is the main idea of this paragraph?

Ⓐ More foreign people began to work in U.S. factories.

Ⓑ In 1880, people from a different part of Europe began to come to the United States.

Ⓒ A large part of the U.S. work force was made up of European immigrants.

Ⓓ People from western Europe stopped coming to the United States.

Questions 14–16 are based on the following passage.

Martin Luther King, Jr., (1929–1968) was an important civil rights leader. He helped to end segregation and to protect the right of African-American people to vote. King won the Nobel Peace Prize in 1964.

King protested for social change in a nonviolent way. He and his followers had peaceful sit-in demonstrations and protest marches. These nonviolent protest methods led to new laws to promote social change. King was assassinated on April 4, 1968. The man who had preached nonviolence suffered a violent death.

14. As a result of the nonviolent demonstrations and protests led by Dr. Martin Luther King, Jr.,

Ⓐ he won the Nobel Peace Prize in 1964.

Ⓑ new laws were passed to promote social change.

Ⓒ segregation increased.

Ⓓ both A and B

15. Martin Luther King, Jr., won the Nobel Peace Prize

Ⓐ before he died.

Ⓑ the same year he died.

Ⓒ after his death.

Ⓓ in 1929.

16. Which method of protest is not nonviolent?

Ⓐ sit-in demonstrations

Ⓑ protest marches

Ⓒ assassination of political leaders

Ⓓ peace marches

Question 17 is based on the chart to the right.

17. Before 1972, only Americans over the age of 21 could vote. In 1972, the law was changed to allow ages 18–21 to vote. From this chart, you can infer that young adults

Ⓐ are less likely to vote than older people.

Ⓑ are as likely to vote as older people.

Ⓒ are more likely to vote than older people.

Ⓓ usually vote for the candidate their parents support.

Voting in U.S. Presidential Elections

Year	Candidates	Percent of Voting Age Population Who Voted
1960	Kennedy* – Nixon	62.8
1964	Johnson* – Goldwater	61.9
1968	Humphrey – Nixon*	60.9
1972	McGovern – Nixon*	55.2
1976	Carter* – Ford	53.5
1980	Carter – Reagan*	54.0
1984	Mondale – Reagan*	53.1
1988	Dukakis – Bush*	50.2
1992	Clinton* – Bush – Perot	55.9

*Starred candidate won.

Questions 18–20 are based on the following paragraph.

The Trobriand Islands are in the South Pacific Ocean, northeast of Australia. The people who live there believe that fathers are not biologically related to their children. They believe that only mothers and the mothers' blood relatives are related to the children. Since the mother's brother is a blood relative, he is the main male figure in the children's life. This uncle passes his social position and property on to his sister's children.

18. The main idea of this paragraph is

Ⓐ the Trobriand Islands are in the South Pacific.

Ⓑ the women in the Trobriand Islands are important.

Ⓒ Trobriand people believe that only mothers and mothers' blood relatives are related to children.

Ⓓ all of the above

19. Which statement best summarizes the paragraph?

Ⓐ Children in the Trobriand Islands don't have any contact with adult males.

Ⓑ People in the South Pacific don't value parents.

Ⓒ Trobriand women depend only on their uncles to care for their children.

Ⓓ The main male figure in the life of a Trobriand child is the brother of the child's mother.

20. How do the roles of males in the Trobriand Islands and in North America compare?

Ⓐ The brothers of Trobriand women play a role similar to that of North American fathers.

Ⓑ Fathers in both the Trobriand Islands and North America pass their property on to their children.

Ⓒ Neither Trobriand Islanders nor North Americans view fathers as blood relatives.

Ⓓ Neither Trobriand Islanders nor North Americans know the difference between a father and an uncle.

When you finish *Check What You've Learned*, check your answers on pages 171-173. Then complete the chart on page 151.

Check What You've Learned

The chart shows you which skills you should go back and review.
Reread each question you missed. Then look at the appropriate
pages of the book for help in figuring out the right answers.

Skills Review Chart

Skills	Questions	Pages
The test, like this book, focuses on the skills below.	Check (√) the questions you missed.	Review what you learned in this book.
Reading Maps	_____ 7 _____ 9	UNIT 1 ◆ Pages 15–44 Strategy for Success Pages 26–27
Making Inferences	_____ 6 _____ 11 _____ 17	UNIT 1 ◆ Pages 15–44 Strategy for Success Pages 38–39
Understanding Time Order	_____ 5 _____ 15	UNIT 2 ◆ Pages 45–74 Strategy for Success Pages 54–55
Compare and Contrast	_____ 8 _____ 16 _____ 20	UNIT 2 ◆ Pages 45–74 Strategy for Success Pages 62–63
Drawing Conclusions	_____ 3 _____ 9 _____ 10	UNIT 3 ◆ Pages 75–90 Strategy for Success Pages 82–83
Cause and Effect	_____ 4 _____ 14	UNIT 4 ◆ Pages 91–120 Strategy for Success Pages 100–101
Facts and Opinions	_____ 7 _____ 12	UNIT 4 ◆ Pages 91–120 Strategy for Success Pages 110–111
Finding the Main Idea	_____ 13 _____ 18	UNIT 5 ◆ Pages 121–143 Strategy for Success Pages 128–129
Summarizing	_____ 19	UNIT 5 ◆ Pages 121–143 Strategy for Success Pages 134–135

absorb To take up or soak up. *page 22*

addiction A need for something that is habit-forming like cigarettes, alcohol, or drugs. *page 138*

affordable housing Homes for people with low incomes. *page 141*

amendment A change or addition. *page 93*

American Revolution The war between the colonists and the English government (1775–1783). *page 52*

Arctic Area surrounding the North Pole and including some of northern Europe. *page 34*

arms race A build-up of weapons where one nation tries to have more than another. *page 71*

article A section of the Constitution. *page 93*

assembly line A line of factory workers and equipment where each worker does a specific job. *page 79*

associate To connect two ideas or events in one's mind. *page 136*

baby boom A period of increased American births (1946–1965). *page 66*

bar graph A graph that uses bars to compare the size of figures. *page 85*

barter system System of trade without use of money. *page 76*

bill An idea for a law that is presented to Congress. *page 98*

Bill of Rights The part of the Constitution that lists people's rights. *page 94*

board of supervisors The government of a county. *page 103*

body language A way of communicating feelings without speaking, for example, by using the face or moving the body. *page 123*

bond A certificate of debt that guarantees repayment of the loan plus interest in a certain period of time. *page 89*

boom A time of rapid economic growth. *page 59*

boundary A dividing line, or border, between areas. *page 18*

branch A part or section. *page 93*

budget A plan to manage money. *page 88*. A yearly plan that shows how much money will come in from taxes, fees, and grants and how the money will be spent. *page 103*

cabinet The group of people who advise the President. *page 97*

candidate A person who seeks to be elected to office. *page 106*

censorship The act of preventing people from expressing their views. *page 94*

census An official count of all the people living in a country. *page 97*

Central America The countries between Mexico and South America. *page 28*

challenge To question or disagree with. *page 48*

chart Information given in the form of a picture or list. *page 84*

city council The law-making body of a city. *page 104*

civil rights The basic rights which every citizen is entitled to. *page 116*

civil war A war between two groups of people in the same country. *page 57*

claim To state one's right of ownership. *page 48*

climate The average weather conditions in a particular place. *page 22*

Cold War The struggle between the United States and the Soviet Union. *page 65*

colony A group of people who settle in another country but remain under the control of the parent country. *page 48*

column A list of information that goes from the top to the bottom of a chart. *page 84*

commission A small group of elected lawmakers. *page 104*

communal Refers to a group of related and unrelated people who live together and share among themselves. *page 125*

communism A system of government where the state controls industry and business, and all goods are shared equally by the people. *page 65*

compass The part of a map that shows the four directions: north, south, east, and west. *page 19*

Confederacy The South during the Civil War. *page 57*

conference committee A special group of five members from each house that recommends the final form of a bill. *page 113*

Congress A formal meeting of representatives to discuss problems. *page 52*

conquistador Spanish word for *conqueror. page 47*

Constitution A document that outlines the system and laws of the United States government. *page 92*

Consumer Price Index A measure of U. S. inflation which shows changes in the prices of goods and services. *page 86*

continent One of the seven large areas of land on the earth. *page 16*

convention A meeting at which members of a political party choose their candidates. *page 106*

county The largest division of an American state. *page 103*

culture The beliefs and ways of doing things in a society. *page 123*

debate To discuss something from different points of view. *page 113*

debtor A person who owes money and can't pay it back. *page 50*

Declaration of Independence The colonies' formal announcement of freedom from the English government. *page 52*

declare To say publicly. *page 57*

deficit When the amount of money the government spends is more than it gets in taxes. *page 88*

democracy Government by the people of a country, either directly or through their elected representatives. *page 116*

depression A long period of severe economic decline. pages 59 and 77. Also, an emotional disorder marked by extreme or prolonged sadness. *page 131*

discriminating Treating people in unequal and unfair ways. *page 117*

economist Someone who specializes in the study of economics. *page 76*

economy The production, distribution, and use of money, goods, natural resources, and services in a country. *page 71*

electoral college A special group of voters from each state that elects the President and Vice-president. *page 106*

electors Members of the electoral college. *page 106*

Emancipation Proclamation The law that freed the slaves in the South. *page 57*

environment Everything that surrounds an animal or person. *page 136*

equator An imaginary line around the middle of the earth. *page 23*

executive branch The President and his or her cabinet. This branch is in charge of making sure that laws are carried out. *page 97*

export To sell and send goods to other countries. *page 30*

family A social group made up of people who are part of one household and are usually related to each other. *page 125*

fertile Very good for growing large, healthy crops. *page 31*

fifteenth century The period from 1401 to 1500. *page 46*

found To start or establish. *page 50*

free state Any state where slavery wasn't allowed. *page 57*

government The method of running a country, state, or city. *page 92*

graph A drawing that shows the relationship between numbers. *page 84*

grassland A large area of grass such as a plain. *page 36*

grief Deep sadness. *page 130*

hemisphere Half of the world. *Hemi-* means "half." A *sphere* is a ball, or a globe. *page 16*

highlands Land that is higher than land near the ocean. *page 42*

homeless Without a permanent address. *page 140*

hormones Substances made in the body. When released into the bloodstream they affect body organs. *page 122*

House of Representatives One of the two houses of Congress. *page 96*

ice cap A permanent cover of thick ice. *page 42*

import To buy and bring foreign goods into a country. *page 30*

industrialized An area that is industrialized has many factories. *page 34*

inflation An economic situation in which the prices of goods and services keep increasing and the value of money keeps decreasing. *page 76*

interest The amount it costs to borrow money. *page 89*

internalize To personally accept and use the norms and values of a society. *page 126*

judicial branch The courts; the branch of government that makes sure laws are constitutional. *page 98*

key Usually a box on a map that explains what the different lines and symbols on the map mean. *page 19*

law of supply and demand The relationship between the supply of goods and the consumer's demand for them. *page 76*

legislative branch Congress; it has the power to make laws. *page 96*

legislator A member of a legislature. *page 102*

legislature The branch of government that makes laws. *page 102*

line graph A graph that uses a line to show an increase or decrease in numbers. *page 85*

majority rule A situation in which over half the people agree on the system or laws of government. *page 94*

merchant Businessperson who buys and sells things. *page 46*

mineral A solid substance, like stone, coal, or salt, that is found in the earth. *page 28*

minimum wage The lowest hourly wage allowed to be paid a U.S. worker. *page 140*

minority The smaller of two groups. *page 116*

Minuteman A civilian who was ready to fight at any time. *page 52*

model To set an example. *page 123*

modify To change. *page 137*

moisture Water in the air that often turns into rain or snow. *page 22*

monsoon A wind in southern Asia. It brings heavy rains to this area each year. *page 40*

natural resources Things found in nature, such as land, water, forests, and minerals. *page 34*

nervous system The body system made up of the brain, spinal cord, and nerves. *page 122*

New Deal The program created by the Roosevelt government to get the U.S. economy out of the depression. *page 60*

nicotine The addictive substance in tobacco. *page 138*

norm The ideas and informal rules shared by the members of a social group. *page 122*

Northwest Passage A sea route through North America to Asia. *page 48*

Office of Management and Budget A government agency that manages the money the government collects. *page 88*

ordinance A law passed by a local government that affects only the city, county, or area controlled by that government. *page 104*

petition A formal request, usually written. *page 116*

phobia An unfounded or extreme fear. *page 131*

pie graph A graph that uses wedge-shaped "slices" to compare a part to the whole. *page 86*

Pilgrims A religious group that settled the Plymouth Colony. *page 50*

plain A large area of flat land. *page 28*

policy The way a business is managed; the rules of a business. *page 118*

poll A place where people vote. *page 106*

preamble The introduction to the Constitution. *page 93*

press News that is published in newspapers, magazines, radio or television. *page 94*

primary An election where voters choose a candidate. *page 106*

productivity The amount produced based on the number of people needed to make the product. *page 79*

protest To fight or speak out against something. *page 68*

public hearing A meeting where members of the public are invited to give their opinion. *page 112*

public works Projects such as roads, bridges, or dams paid for by the government for the people's use. *page 64*

punishment A way to discourage a type of behavior. *page 136*

rain forest A wet tropical forest with tall trees that grow very close together. *page 31*

random Having no particular order or pattern. *page 136*

raw material A natural substance, like cotton or wood, from which goods are made. *page 32*

rebel To struggle against authority. *page 68*

recession A decline in economic activity. *page 77*

referendum A chance for voters to approve or reject laws. *page 103*

reform An effort to improve. *page 72*

refugees People who flee a place because of disaster or war. *page 68*

reinforcement A way to encourage a type of behavior. *page 136*

representative A person who voices the needs, wants, and opinions of a group of people. *page 92*

republic A country whose leader is elected by the people. *page 72*

revolt To rebel against authority. *page 71*

robot A computerized machine that does the same work as a human. *page 80*

role An expected way of behaving. *page 123*

row A list of information that goes from left to right across a chart. *page 84*

scale A line in the map key that helps measure the distances on the map. *page 20*

secede To leave a group or organization officially. *page 57*

Second World War World War II, fought between England, the United States, and their allies on one side and Germany, Italy, Japan, and their allies on the other (1939–1945). *page 64*

segregation Social separation of different groups of people. *page 57.* Separating people on the basis of race. *page 117*

Senate One of the two houses of Congress. *page 96*

settle To make a home. *page 46*

shelter A temporary dwelling for homeless persons. *page 141*

shortage Not enough of something to meet demand. *page 76*

socialization The process of learning the rules of behavior of a social group. *page 122*

sponsor To present a bill and take responsibility for it. *page 112*

standing committee A group of senators or representatives who deal with a special topic such as agriculture or foreign relations. *page 112*

stock A share that a person owns in a company. *page 59*

stock market The place where stocks are bought and sold. *page 59*

stress Emotional tension. *page 131*

subject The animal or person that is being studied in an experiment. *page 136*

surrender To give oneself or one's army to the enemy. *page 52*

symbol A person or thing that stands for an idea. *page 108*

system of checks and balances The system that keeps the different branches of government from getting too powerful. *page 98*

table To set aside debate on a bill for a while. *page 112*

tariff A tax on imports or exports. *page 30*

term The period of time for which a person holds office. *page 107*

tourism Traveling for pleasure. *page 31*

trading post A store set up by merchants or traders. *page 50*

trend A general direction of growth or change. *page 86*

Union The North during the Civil War. *page 57*

values The ideas that a society considers to be most important. *page 122*

veto The power of the president to reject a bill. *page 98*

welfare Money paid by the government to people who need help. *page 64*

withdrawal A physical or emotional response to giving up a drug. *page 138*

Answers and Explanations

Check What You Know

Page 7

1. **(D) after the English took over.** The last sentence tells that the English named the old Dutch colony New York. Choice A is incorrect because the Indians called it Manhattan. Choices B and C are incorrect because, before the English had the colony, the Dutch called it New Amsterdam.

2. **(D) all of the above.** The English colony of New York was called Manhattan by the Indians and New Amsterdam by the Dutch when it was a Dutch colony.

Page 8

3. **(D) The President is elected and the Supreme Court justices are appointed.** Choice A is not true. Choice B is incorrect because the passage says nothing about the age of the President in relation to the Supreme Court justices. Choice C is incorrect because justices of the Supreme Court have their jobs for life or until they decide to retire.

4. **(C) The President should consult leaders in Congress before choosing a Supreme Court justice.** Although Congress must approve appointments, there is no requirement that the President consult Congressional leaders beforehand. However, some politicians have that opinion. Choices A, B, and D are facts stated in the passage.

Page 9

5. **(A) the President and the justices might not always agree.** You can conclude that the President and the justices don't always agree since the President has to work with justices appointed by other Presidents. Choices B, C, and D are incorrect because there is no reason to conclude that the President will be friendly with justices appointed by other Presidents.

6. **(B) The U.S. government has a system of checks and balances.** This passage gives an example of how the system of checks and balances works. Choice A is not true. Choices C and D are facts that support the main idea.

7. **(C) the size and location of North America's deserts.** The map shows the areas covered by the deserts. Choices A, B, and D are incorrect because the map does not show information about temperature and rainfall or plants and animals.

Page 10

8. **(D) both B and C.** Since Montana's products include farm crops, range animals, lumber, and metals, you can conclude that the state has farms, ranches, forests, and mines. Choice A is incorrect because the map does not show information about factories.

9. **(C) Metals come from the middle and western parts of Montana.** The symbol for metals appears on the middle and western parts of the map. Choice A is incorrect because lettuce and strawberries are not shown on the map. Choice B is incorrect because poultry and wheat come from different areas. Choice D is not true.

10. **(B) Montana is rich in resources.** The fact that there are so many products scattered throughout the state indicates that the state is rich in resources. Choice A is incorrect

because the map doesn't provide any information about how profitable lumber and ranching businesses are. Choice C is incorrect because the map doesn't tell about working conditions for miners.

Page 11

11. **(B) helping big businesses would help the whole economy.** The fourth sentence explains that Reagan wanted to help the whole economy grow by helping big business. Choice A is not what the Reagan administration thought. Choice C is incorrect because the passage never states that banks didn't want to help people. Choice D is not a reason for helping big businesses.

12. **(A) The government helped big businesses but not small ones.** Sentences 1–3 explain how the Reagan Administration helped big businesses. Choices B and C are incorrect because the government did not help small businesses. Choice D is incorrect because the government made conditions worse for small businesses, but better for big businesses.

13. **(D) President Reagan's idea that helping big business would help the whole economy did more harm than good.** This is an opinion based on the facts in the passage. Opinions can not be proven true. The other choices are facts stated in the passage.

Page 12

14. **(A) expand German territory.** Since the passage explains that Hitler wanted to expand German territory, it is logical that invading Poland was an effort to do this. Choice B is incorrect because nothing in the passage indicates that Poland had a dictator. Choices C and D are incorrect because invading Poland didn't help Japan or Italy.

15. **(B) World War II began because Hitler wanted to expand Germany's territory.** The other choices are supporting details that explain how Hitler's effort to expand Germany led to the war.

16. **(D) Japan attacked Pearl Harbor.** The third paragraph explains that the United States stayed out of the war until 1941, when Pearl Harbor was attacked. Choices A and C are incorrect because these events happened after the United States entered the war. Choice B took place two years before the United States entered the war.

Page 13

17. **(B) when Japan surrendered.** The fourth paragraph explains that Japan's surrender ended the war. The other choices took place before the end of the war.

18. **(C) closed and open societies are different.** The passage discusses differences between closed and open societies. Choices B and D are details from the passage. Choice A is incorrect because achievement is only mentioned in the passage but is not explained.

19. **(B) People in open societies can change their social status, but people in closed societies cannot.** The other choices are opinions, and they do not summarize the information in the passage.

20. (C) can't change the social status they are born with. The first paragraph says that people have the status of their parents when they are born. The last paragraph says that people in a closed society can't change their status through achievement. Choice A is true in an open society, but not in a closed society. Choices B and D are not true in either an open or a closed society.

Unit 1 ◆ Lesson 1

Page 18

There are many ways to answer the questions. Share your work with your teacher.

Page 21

1. key
2. continents
3. boundary
4. Eastern Hemisphere, Europe
5. Antarctica
6. **(A) the oceans.** Choices B, C, and D are incorrect because they cover less area.
7. **(B) The earth's land is divided into continents.** Choices A is incorrect because water covers three-fourths of the earth's surface. Choice B is incorrect because a globe shows one-half of the earth at a time. Choice D is incorrect because there are seven continents.

Lesson 2

Page 25

1. equator
2. moisture
3. climate
4. The climate is hot and wet.
5. In the northern part of Asia, you would wear very warm clothing because it is cold.

Pages 26–27

Exercise 1: 1. 4,500

2. 2,000

Exercise 2: 1. hot and wet; desert; warm summers and cool or cold winters

2. desert

3. (B) along the northern coast. Choice A is incorrect because central Australia has a desert climate. Choices C and D are incorrect because the southern coast has a climate with only medium rainfall. It is not considered a "wet" climate.

Lesson 3

Page 33

1. export
2. plains
3. fertile
4. Chile and Argentina
5. 40–79 inches
6. **(B) South America.** Choices A, C, and D are incorrect because the equator does not pass through North America, Central America, or the Caribbean Sea.

7. (D) Canada and the United States. Choices A, B, and C are incorrect because Mexico is not one of the two countries that make more than one-fourth of the world's manufactured goods.

Lesson 4

Page 37

1. grassland
2. industrialized
3. Arctic
4. Uganda, Tanzania, Kenya
5. Tanzania
6. Kenya
7. Uganda, Rwanda, Burundi, Zaire, Zambia

Pages 38–39
Exercise 1: Europe and the United States are nearly the same size.

Three times as many people live in Europe as in the United states.

Exercise 2: (B) There is probably less open land in Europe than in the United States. Choices A and C are incorrect because if Europe and the United States are the same size and if more people live in Europe, the land available for people to live on in Europe is probably more crowded.

Exercise 3: There are many possible ways to answer the question. Here is an example.

Deserts do not get much rain. Deserts are hot during the day. Without water in the desert, people get thirsty and plants die.

Farmers need a dependable amount of rain to grow food.

Exercise 4: (C) Large parts of Africa cannot be farmed. Choice A is incorrect because deserts, which do not get much rain and are therefore not suited for farming, cover a large portion of Africa. Choice B is incorrect because deserts would not have a problem with floods. Choice D is incorrect because the passage does not support the choice.

Exercise 5: More than two-fifths of Africa is desert.

Lesson 5

Page 43

1. Atlantic Ocean, Indian Ocean, Pacific Ocean
2. The South Pole
3. **(D) all of the above.** Choices A, B, and C are only partial answers.
4. **(A) sparsely populated.** Choices B, C, and D are incorrect since the interior and western parts of the country are unlikely to be either crowded or noisy if most of the people live along the east coast. Therefore, it is also unlikely that these areas will be filled with shopping malls or be important business centers.
5. **(C) a wind that brings heavy rain.** The text says that monsoons are seasonal winds. All other choices do not refer to wind.

Page 44
There are many ways to answer questions 1–3. Here are some examples.

1. A map can tell you the climate of a place; how many people live there; the location or size of a body of water or land; and the distance between cities.

2. Geography can tell you how many people live in an area; the languages they speak; the types of houses they live in; how they get food or make money to live.

3. Climate affects what types of clothes people wear. It can affect what kinds of houses people live in and how they get from place to place.

4. There are many ways to answer the question. Share your work with your teacher.

Unit 2 ◆ Lesson 6

Page 48

There are many possible ways to answer the question. Share your work with your teacher.

Page 49

1. claim

2. challenge

3. merchant

4. **(B) valuable.** Choices A, C, and D are incorrect because merchants would not have traveled so far to get things that were plentiful, thin, or cheap.

5. **(A) a way by ship.** Choices B and D are incorrect because the term says nothing about the length of a trip. Choice C is incorrect because merchants could already reach India by land.

6. **(C) a trip by ship would be easier and faster.** Choice A is incorrect because merchants did not care whether or not the world was round. Choice B is incorrect because they could already get there by land. Choice D is incorrect because they did not know the Americas existed.

Lesson 7

Page 53

1. Debtors, Pilgrims

2. surrendered

3. **(B) taxes.** Choices A, C, and D cannot be raised or charged on products as the paragraph states.

4. **(C) stop trading with.** Choices A and B are incorrect because the next sentence says the colonists decided to stop trading with the British. Choice D is incorrect because if a boycott was an act against the British, then its meaning is opposite of *to meet with*.

5. **(B) wanted to be free to practice their religion.** Choice A is incorrect because governors and merchants got rich in the colonies. Choice C is incorrect because debtors were sent to the colonies as a punishment. Choice D is incorrect because merchants owned trading posts in the colonies.

6. **(C) colonists decided on a plan of action against England.** Choice A is incorrect because the first Congress met in Philadelphia. Choice B is incorrect because men from 12, or nearly all of the original 13, colonies met. Choice D is incorrect because the Declaration of Independence was not signed until 1776, and the first Congress met in 1774.

Pages 54–55

Exercise 1: In 1492, Christopher Columbus began his first trip across the Atlantic Ocean in search of India. After that first trip, he went back three more times. When he died in 1505, he still had not found a route to India. It wasn't until much <u>later</u> that people realized the importance of his discoveries.

Exercise 2: (B) Choice B is correct because these events happened over seven years in a specific order. Choice A does not involve time order.

Exercise 3: There are many ways to answer the question. Here is an example.

For seven years, Columbus tried to find someone to pay for his trips. First, he asked John II of Portugal for money. After that, he wrote to Henry VI of England. Finally, he met with Spain's Queen Isabella.

Lesson 8

Page 58

1. secede

2. civil

3. **(D) both A and B.** Choice C is incorrect because the Confederate States fought in the Civil War.

4. **(B) during the Civil War.** Choice A is incorrect because the Emancipation Proclamation was issued in 1863 and the war began in 1861. Choice C is incorrect because the Confederacy did not surrender until 1865. Choice D is incorrect because Lincoln was not President during the 1850s.

5. **(C) for another hundred years after the Civil War.** Choices A and B are incorrect because these dates mark the beginning and ending of the Civil War, not segregation. Choice D is incorrect because this event ended the Civil War, but not segregation.

6. **(B) some slave states.** Choice A is incorrect because four slave states stayed in the Union. Choices C and D are incorrect because none of the free states joined the Confederacy.

Lesson 9

Page 61

1. stock

2. boom

3. depression

4. **(A) after the stock market crash of 1929.** Choices B and D are incorrect because both were responses to the Depression. Choice C is incorrect because the Depression began in 1929.

5. **(C) during the Great Depression.** Choices A and D are incorrect because Roosevelt told voters he had a plan to help end the Depression. Choice B is incorrect because Black Tuesday was the day of the stock market crash that began the Great Depression.

6. **(C) watch over.** Choices A, B, and C would not help ensure that there would never be another crash.

Pages 62–63

Exercise 1: worst; unlike

Exercise 2: worst

Exercise 3: In the 1920s businesses made large <u>profits</u>. The 1930s were not the <u>same</u>, (however). Business failures were (unlike) they had ever been before. The depression was just <u>as</u> bad for farmers <u>as</u> for people in the <u>cities</u>. Many farmers lost their farms and were barely able to grow enough to eat.

Exercise 4: Roosevelt's New Deal was (like) a rope <u>thrown to drowning people</u>. Government began to play a role in people's lives (more) than ever before. The government created a safety net that made sure there would never be another depression. Some Americans think <u>Roosevelt</u> was one of the (best) <u>presidents the United States ever had</u>.

Exercise 5: There are many possible ways to answer the question. Here are two examples.

- During the Great Depression, many people went without food and had no place to live. Though Americans experience homelessness and hunger today, it is not as bad as it was then.

- More people are employed today than during the depression. Back then, about 13 million Americans were without jobs.

Lesson 10

Page 67

1. Welfare

2. communism

3. **(A) the United States felt threatened by the Soviets.** Choice B is incorrect because the United States and the Soviet Union did not work together after the war. Choices C and D are incorrect because the Soviet Union continued to be very important, but it was not the most powerful nation in the world.

4. **(C) their cities, factories, and fields were in ruins.** Choice A is incorrect because the Americans did not force them to rebuild. Choice B is incorrect because battles were also fought in the Pacific area. Choice D is incorrect because selling goods was not the main reason for rebuilding.

5. **(B) after the war, many Americans started families.** Choice A is incorrect because immigration was not the major cause of the population increase. Choices C is incorrect because lack of travel would increase the population. Choice D is incorrect because the government did not encourage people to have children.

Lesson 11

Page 70

1. protested

2. refugees

3. Hanoi

4. Laos, Cambodia

5. **(C) when the Viet Cong rebelled against the government in the south.** Choices A and B are incorrect because these events took place before the Vietnam War. Choice D is incorrect because the United States didn't send troops until after the war had already started.

6. **(A) before South Vietnam surrendered.** Choice B happened before United States troops left Vietnam. Choice C is incorrect because United States troops did not win the war. Choice D happened after United States troops left Vietnam.

Lesson 12

Page 73

1. economy

2. republics

3. revolted

4. **(B) when Gorbachev resigned from office.** Choices A, C and D all happened before the end of the Soviet Union.

5. **(B) when communism fell in East Germany.** Choices A and D took place before the Berlin Wall was opened. Choice C took place after the Berlin Wall was opened.

6. **(D) all of the above**

Page 74

1. There are many possible ways to answer the question. Share your work with your teacher.

2. There are many possible ways to answer the question. Share your work with your teacher.

3. There are many possible ways to answer the question. Here is an example.

    The main reason for fighting the American Revolution was to gain freedom from England. The colonists no longer wanted to be ruled unfairly by King George III. The Civil War happened because the Union did not want to allow the South to secede from the nation. The great differences between the two halves of the country caused the war. The Vietnam War broke out because of the fight between the Communists and non-Communists. The United States became involved to help the non-Communists.

4. There are many possible ways to answer the question. Share your work with your teacher.

Unit 3 ◆ Lesson 13

Page 78

1. depression

2. economist

3. barter

4. shortage

5. **(D) wages and prices go up.** Choices A, B, and C are incorrect because neither wages nor prices go down during an inflation.

6. **(B) business slows down and people lose their jobs.** Choice A

is incorrect because businesses do not grow during a recession. Choice C is incorrect because people do not have money to spend during a recession. Choice D is incorrect because prices don't necessarily go up during a recession.

7. **(A) shells, stones, and beads.** Choices B and C are incorrect because neither cloth, pottery, diamonds, or gold were commonly used as early forms of money. Choice D is incorrect because goods and services are not forms of money.

Lesson 14

Page 80

There are many possible ways to answer the question. Here is an example.

Computers allow people to program wristwatch alarms and appliances such as microwave ovens. Computers also allow people to get money and make deposits after banking hours. They help people keep track of information.

Page 81

1. productivity

2. robot

3. twelve and a half, fewer

4. $850, down

5. **(A) after interchangeable parts were invented.** Choice B is incorrect because assembly lines require interchangeable parts. Choice C is incorrect because robots were invented after assembly lines. Choice D is incorrect because wagons are a very old form of technology that was used long before the assembly line.

6. (D) in the 1970s. Choices A and B are incorrect because the times mentioned are well before factories started using robots. Choice C is incorrect because Henry Ford began using the assembly line before robots were used.

Pages 82–83

Exercise 1: One of the ways that factories use robots is to do dangerous jobs. People should not have to do jobs in which they can be injured. Robots can be used to do high-temperature welding. There may be sparks from the welding, but robots won't get burned. They are made of metal. Sometimes humans can be careless and hurt someone. Robots do what they are programmed to do. You can't say that a robot is ever careless!

(B) Using robots reduces the chance of human workers being injured.
Choices A and C are incorrect because they are not supported by information in the passage.

Exercise 2: The Great Depression followed a time of economic boom. In 1929, many stocks were worth three times what they were worth in 1924. Then in October 1929, stock prices dropped suddenly. Stock prices continued to fall for the next year and a half. Some people who owned stock had no other form of savings. When the value of their stock went down, they were left without money. As a result, many businesses failed.

Unemployment increased during the depression. In 1930, there were four million unemployed Americans. By 1933, the number had grown to over 14 million. Many people in cities had no money and no jobs. Some people died of starvation. Others left cities to look for work in other places. More than two million people moved from cities to farm areas, hoping to find jobs and food.

The government tried many programs to ease the problems of the depression. While these did help in some places, the problems of unemployment continued through most of the 1930s.

1. Stock prices went up, then down.

2. This conclusion can be based on the facts in the first 4 sentences of the passage.

3. Unemployment increased during the 1930s.

Lesson 15

Page 87

1. pie

2. trend

3. row

4. **(B) lived in cities.** Choices A and D are incorrect because most Americans did not live or work on farms. Choice C is incorrect because the chart says nothing about where people who lived in cities worked.

5. **(C) more money today than they did in either 1970 or 1980.** Choices A, B and D are incorrect because the cost of goods and services has gone up since both 1970 and 1980.

6. **(A) A chart usually gives more exact numbers than a graph.** Choice B is incorrect because graphs show the overall picture of a trend better. Choice C is incorrect because this statement compares two kinds of graphs, not a chart and a graph. Choice D is incorrect because it is a personal judgement not a factual difference.

Lesson 16

Page 89
There are many possible ways to answer the question. Share your work with your teacher.

Page 90
1. interest

2. budget

3. deficit

4. **(B) taxes on personal and business income.** Choice A is incorrect because the government pays interest on the public debt; it doesn't receive the interest. Choice C is incorrect because most of the money from sales of goods goes to the businesses that make the goods. Choice D is incorrect because choices A and C are incorrect.

5. **(A) after the President has asked for a new budget.** Choices B, C, and D are incorrect because the OMB makes its budget before Congress votes and before the collection of all taxes.

6. **(B) after the government interest rate goes up.** Choice A is incorrect because bank interest rates change in response to changes in the federal interest rate. Choice C is incorrect because the number of customers doesn't necessarily affect interest rates. Choice D is incorrect because the existence of a deficit doesn't directly affect interest rates.

Unit 4 ◆ Lesson 17

Page 95
1. government

2. Constitution

3. amendments

4. There are many ways to answer the question. Here is an example.

   The authors of the Bill of Rights wanted to protect minority rights because they wanted to create a government that provided freedom for all people.

5. **(A) People of a country should have the power to make their own laws.** Choice B is incorrect because the authors of the Constitution believed that the government's powers needed to be limited. Choice C is incorrect because federal laws need to be stronger than state laws to maintain order and to hold the country together. Choice D is not true and is not mentioned in the text as a basis for the Constitution.

6. **(C) Each branch could keep the other two from becoming too powerful.** Choice A is incorrect because the amount of work to do was not an issue. Choice B is incorrect because the issue of who would govern was not a factor in this decision. Choice D is incorrect because the branches do not represent geographic regions.

Lesson 18

Page 99
1. Senate

2. veto

3. judicial

4. **(B) after the census is taken.** Choice A is incorrect because the census must be taken first to determine the number of people to be represented. Choice C is incorrect because the census must be completed. Choice D is incorrect

because the census is taken once every ten years.

5. **(B) after the President appoints them.** Choice A is incorrect because they must be appointed first. Choice C is incorrect because they must be approved before they can serve. Choice D cannot be correct for the above reasons.

6. There are many ways to answer the question. Here is an example.

The President can send a bill to Congress. But only Congress can make bills into law. However, the President has the power to reject a bill that the Congress has passed. The Congress and the President must work together because they share power and responsibility for getting bills passed.

Pages 100–101
Exercise 1: There are many possible ways to rewrite these sentences. Here is an example.
Because the Constitution was carefully written, it is still a useful plan of government today.
Exercise 2: The key word *so* should be circled.
Exercise 3: There are many possible ways to rewrite these sentences. Here is an example.
Some people were afraid that the federal government might be given too much power. As a result, the writers of the Constitution split the federal government into three branches.
Exercise 4:

1. yes

2. yes

Exercise 5: There are many ways to answer the questions. Share your work with your teacher.

Lesson 19

Page 105

1. budget

2. referendum

3. ordinance

4. commission

5. There are many ways to answer the question. Here is an example.

Counties and cities are part of a state so the ordinances they make cannot do anything that violates state laws.

6. because (or since); if

7. Therefore

8. Since (or Because)

Lesson 20

Page 107
There are many ways to answer the question. Share your work with your teacher.

Page 109

1. candidate, primary

2. terms

3. symbols

4. **(B) People vote in a primary election.** Choices A and C are incorrect because they take place after the primary elections are completed. Choice D is incorrect because the legislature does not elect the President.

5. **(B) the most voters.** A presidential candidate who wanted to win would try to campaign where he or she could get the most votes. Choices A and C are incorrect because natural resources and historic buildings can't vote. Choice D is incorrect because unemployment

rates could be high in a state with very few voters.

6. **(A) current events.** Choice B is incorrect because political cartoons are about events in the news, not events in past history. Choice C is incorrect because the animals in political cartoons are symbols, not the subject of the cartoons. Choice D is incorrect because political cartoons can be about any current subject, not just the president.

Pages 110–111
Exercise 1:
1. F 2. F 3. F 4. O 5. F 6. O 7. O
Exercise 2: Opinion: The Electoral College is not democratic. Facts: Candidates who won most votes in 1824, 1876, and 1888 were not chosen by the Electoral College.
Exercise 3: There are many possible ways to answer the question. Here is an example.
Fact 1: Delegates from a party vote for presidential and vice-presidential candidates.
Fact 2: Geraldine Ferraro was the first woman chosen as a vice-presidential candidate from a major party.
Opinion: There should be a woman chosen as a presidential candidate from a major party in the next election.

Lesson 21

Page 115

1. sponsor
2. standing
3. debate
4. F
5. O
6. O

7. F
8. **(A) goes to the Senate.** Choice B is incorrect because a bill goes to a conference committee only after a version of it has passed both houses. Choice C is incorrect because the bill goes to a standing committee before it is voted on. Choice D is incorrect because the bill goes to the President only after being passed by both houses.

Lesson 22

Page 119

1. petition
2. segregation
3. policy
4. **(B) The Fourteeth Amendment to the Constitution.** Choice A is incorrect because the 1875 decision restored legal segregation. Choice C is incorrect because this amendment gave African-American men the right to vote. Choice D is incorrect because the bus boycott occurred in the 1950s, long after African Americans had won citizenship.
5. F
6. O
7. O

Page 120

1. There are many possible ways to answer the question. Here is an example. The Constitution makes sure that no one person gets too much power by establishing a systems of checks and balances, giving rights to the people and states, and having leaders be elected by the people.

2. There are many possible ways to answer questions 2 and 3. Share your work with your teacher.

Unit 5 ◆ Lesson 23

Page 124

1. Hormones

2. socialization

3. value

4. **(C) making sure young family members attend school.** Choices A, B, and D are incorrect because they describe activities or other roles adults may have. They do not describe the parent's role of caring for his or her children.

5. **(B) adrenaline.** Choices A and C are incorrect because these are related to learned behavior. The body's reaction to anger is not learned.

6. **(D) will not learn the norms and the values of society.** Choices A, B, and C are incorrect because people may be socialized, yet not learn group sports, go to college, or be invited to parties.

Lesson 24

Page 127

1. family

2. internalize

3. communal

4. **(C) a mother, father, and five children.** Choice A is incorrect because it does not necessarily describe a family. Choice B describes an extended family. Choice D is incorrect because it describes a single-parent family.

5. **(A) The percentage of single-parent families has grown.** Choice B, is incorrect because the percentage of nuclear families has decreased. Choices C and D are incorrect because the graph does not address whether the family has fallen apart or if more people are starting families.

6. **(D) all of the above.** Choices A, B, and C are only partial answers.

Pages 128–129
Exercise 1: Foster families are temporary families for some children.
Exercise 2: There are many possible ways to answer the question. Here is an example. There are many kinds of families.

Lesson 25

Page 132
There are many possible ways to answer the question. Share your work with your teacher.

Page 133

1. depression

2. phobia

3. stress

4. **(D) all of the above.** The last paragraph on page 131 and the first paragraph on page 132 describe some of the effects and signs of stress. These include depression, high blood pressure, stomach upset, and eating too much.

5. **(C) depression.** The second paragraph on page 131 states that a depressed person may need help from a doctor. Choice A, B, and D are incorrect because these are normal feelings, and most people handle them without treatment.

6. **(C) There are many signs of stress.** Choices A, B, and D are true, but they are the details which support the main idea.

Pages 134–135
Exercise 1: There are many possible ways to answer the questions. Here are some examples.

1. Topic: stress

   Main Idea: Stress is common, but it can lead to physical and emotional problems.

   Important facts: Stress can lead to depression. Stress can lead to stomach problems or high blood pressure. Many people must cope with stress.

2. Stress is a normal problem that many people cope with. However, it can lead to depression, stomach problems, or high blood pressure.

Exercise 2: There are many possible ways to answer the question. Here is an example.

Extreme fears, or phobias, are serious problems that may make it hard for a person to function in society.

Lesson 26

Page 139

1. addiction

2. environment

3. **(C) Behavioral psychologists are interested in the way that people and animals respond to the world they live in.** Choices A and B are the opposite of what is stated in the paragraph.

4. **(C) Positive reinforcement and punishment can be used to modify behavior.** Choices A and B are details that support the main idea. Choice D is an opinion, not a fact.

5. **(B) Praise and rewards are ways of giving positive reinforcement.** Choices A, C, and D are incorrect because they are too specific to summarize the paragraphs.

Lesson 27

Page 142

1. affordable

2. shelters

3. **(B) doctors felt that keeping patients in the hospital for long periods of time did them little good.** Choices A, C, and D may have been true in some cases, but Choice B is stated in the passage as the reason patients were released.

4. **(D) all of the above.** Choices A, B, and C are only partial answers.

5. **(A) Many people are active in trying to fight problems and help make society better.** Choices B, C, and D are true, but they do not summarize the last two paragraphs which talk about positive change.

Page 143
There are many possible ways to answer questions 1 and 2. Here are some examples.

1. By understanding behavior, scientists can find ways to change or influence behavior.

2. Behaviors might include laughing and screaming. There are physical factors behind these behaviors, including the release of adrenaline, and the responses of the nervous system. Learning is also a factor behind these behaviors. People may become socialized to act in certain ways when riding roller coasters. There are many possible ways to answer questions 3 and 4. Share your work with your teacher.

Check What You've Learned

Page 144

1. **(B) Florida.** The southern tip of Florida is in a tropical climate zone. All other choices have hot summers and mild winters.

Page 145

2. **(A) Georgia has mild winters and hot summers.** The map shows Georgia in a zone of mild winters and hot summers. Choice B is incorrect because Maine has warm summers. Choice C is incorrect because the map does not tell how much snow a region gets. Choice D is not true; Pennsylvania and New Jersey have two climate zones, not three.

3. **(D) English.** Paragraph three says that the government, language, and style of dress in Hawaii is American. Since English is the main language used in the United States, we can conclude that English is the main language in Hawaii.

Page 146

4. **(D) both A and B.** The second paragraph states that rich soil and a warm climate make Hawaii ideal for sugar cane, coffee, and pineapples.

5. **(D) after 1900.** The last paragraph states that Hawaii was an American territory between 1900 and 1959. Choices A and B are incorrect because Hawaii was a territory before it became a state in 1959. Choice C is incorrect because this date is before Hawaii became a territory.

6. **(C) people from different cultures live together.** You could infer this because the sentence that calls Hawaii a "melting pot" follows a sentence that says that people from many different cultures live together in Hawaii.

7. **(B) The people who went out west under the Homestead Act were braver than those who stayed in the East.** This statement is an opinion because there is nothing in the passage about the qualities of those who went out west and those who stayed in the East. All other choices are facts stated in the passage.

Page 147

8. **(C) both caused people to move west.** Choice A is incorrect because the Gold Rush was not started by the government. Choice B is incorrect because the Homestead Act was passed in 1862. Choice D is incorrect because the Homestead Act did encourage people to settle down in the west.

9. **(B) 1940 and 1950.** The biggest increase in the height of bars on the graph occurs between 1940 and 1950.

10. **(D) a steady increase in the number of women in the work force.** The height of the bars increases, showing a steady growth in the number of women in the work force over the years.

11. **(C) a higher percentage of children born in 1980 have mothers who work than did children born in 1920.** Choices A, B, and D are incorrect because the graph does not show how much women are paid or how much education they have.

Page 148

12. **(B) After 1880, people began to come to the United States from southern and eastern Europe.** Where people came from at a certain time can be proven. All the other choices are opinions about people's attitudes and feelings.

13. **(B) In 1880, people from a different part of Europe began to come to the United States.** The passage emphasizes the difference between the immigrant populations before and after 1880.

Page 149

14. **(D) both A and B.** King's leadership of a nonviolent civil rights movement caused him to win the Nobel Peace Prize and brought about new laws to promote social change. Choice C is incorrect because King's work helped end segregation, not increase it.

15. **(A) before he died.** The first paragraph says that King won the Nobel Peace Prize in 1964. He died in 1968.

16. **(C) assassination of political leaders.** None of the other methods use acts of violence as a means of protest.

17. **(A) are less likely to vote than older people.** Since the percentage of voter participation went down after younger people became eligible to vote, one can infer that they are less likely to vote than older people. Choices B and C are contradicted by the chart. There is no information to support Choice D.

Page 150

18. **(C) Trobriand people believe that only mothers and mothers' blood relatives are related to children.** Choice A is incorrect because this is a detail, not the main idea. Choice B is not mentioned in the passage.

19. **(D) The main male figure in the life of a Trobriand child is the brother of the child's mother.** Choice A is incorrect because children do have contact with their uncles. Choice B is wrong because the mother is important in determining a child's blood relations. Choice C is wrong because the passage states that a woman is dependent on her brother, not her uncle.

20. **(A) The brothers of Trobriand women play a role similar to that of North American fathers.** Just as North American fathers pass social status and property to their children, Trobriand uncles pass social status and property to their children. Choice

B is incorrect because fathers in the Trobriand Islands do not pass their property to their children. Choice C is incorrect because North Americans do view fathers as blood relatives. Choice D is incorrect because people in both places do know the difference between a father and an uncle.

NORTH
AMERICA

ATLANTIC
OCEAN

PACIFIC
OCEAN

N
W   E
S

Equator

SOUTH
AMERICA

SCALE

0   500   1,000   2,000 MILES